The Action of the
HOLY SPIRIT

THE LORD AND GIVER OF LIFE

The Action of the
HOLY SPIRIT

THE LORD AND GIVER OF LIFE

FRANK J. SHEED

With a Foreword by
Alan Schreck

Originally published in 1981 as *The Holy Spirit in Action:
Why Christians Call Him "The Lord and Giver of Life"* by
Servant Publications

15 14 13 12 11   4 5 6 7 8

The Word Among Us Press
7115 Guilford Drive
Frederick, Maryland 21704
www.wau.org

ISBN: 978-1-59325-070-6

Cover design by DesignWorks

Cover painting, El Greco, (1541-1614) The Pentecost.
Location: Museo del Prado, Madrid, Spain
Photo Credit: Scala/Art Resource, NY

Made and printed in the United States of America

Library of Congress Cataloging-in-Publication Data

Sheed, F. J. (Francis Joseph)
  [Holy Spirit in action]
  The action of the Holy Spirit : the Lord and giver of life / by Frank J. Sheed.
    p. cm.
  Originally published: The Holy Spirit in Action. Ann Arbor, Mich. : Servant
Publications, 1981.
  ISBN 1-59325-070-3 (alk. paper)
  1. Holy Spirit. I. Title.
  BT121.3.S54 2006
  231'.3--dc22
                                                    2005029248

Table of Contents

Foreword

Alan Schreck, PhD
Professor of Theology
Franciscan University of Steubenville

When someone writes a book today on the Holy Spirit, many people—especially Catholics—ask, "Why?" Their "why" could mean either, "Why is the Holy Spirit important?" (which is a good reason for them to read the book) or, "Why does the author want me to learn about the Holy Spirit? Is he/she trying to convert me to something?"

Anyone familiar with Frank Sheed knows what his motive is. This seasoned twentieth-century street apologist simply wants to explain the mysteries of faith to the layperson. And why the Holy Spirit? Because he is one of the greatest and most central mysteries of the Christian faith.

In God, who is spirit, who is this that is simply called *Holy* Spirit? Part I of Sheed's book explores this question—looking at this mysterious "breath" who is also called gift, love, (another) paraclete, and in the Creed, "Lord and giver of life."

This is just the beginning. The book is entitled *The Action of the Holy Spirit*, and Sheed shines in explaining how the Holy Spirit acts in the life of the church and in each Christian. "Action upon mankind, individually and in community, is the special function of the Holy Spirit" is the first line of Part II: The Spirit in Action. "Jesus, we remember, handed over his church on earth to the keeping of the Holy Spirit" opens chapter nine. "We are in the hands of the Spirit," Sheed asserts, but like Jesus, Mary, the apostles, and all the saints, we have to *choose* to allow the Holy Spirit to guide us and act in our lives. This is not always an easy choice, as Sheed notes: "Life can seem so dubiously worth living. That is why in a devitalized age, under the same pressure as everyone else, we should give more mind to the Spirit of Life, the Holy Spirit, with whose life-giving activities both Testaments positively sparkle" (p. 119).

This book is provocative, challenging people to use their "mental muscles" to think about God. The book is solidly grounded in the texts of the Bible that allude to the Spirit—another demonstration that authentic Catholics are, and must become more, a people who know their faith through the sacred texts that God has "breathed" with his Spirit.

Finally, Sheed is a master at the clever turn of phrase and striking image. For instance, after reminding us that the Spirit "reinforces the power of hope," Sheed remarks, "There is no place in hell for even the smallest flickering of love" (p. 115). As long as the Spirit, who is Love, is alive (even "flickering") in us, we have the hope of heaven.

This little book is a good one to introduce you to the Holy Spirit. It will challenge you to think about God, to turn to sacred Scripture, and to pray in order to perceive and follow "the action of the Holy Spirit" in your life.

Prologue

To the apostles, desolated to learn that he was leaving them, Jesus said it was better *for them* that he should go. Why? Because if he did not go, the Holy Spirit would not come. Who or what is the Spirit whose coming could thus be better for them, and better for us, than the bodily presence of Jesus? That is what this book is about.

At his ascension, Jesus, slain and risen from death, told the apostles to stay in Jerusalem till "you shall receive power [*dynamis*] when the Holy Spirit has come upon you; and you shall be my witnesses in Jerusalem and . . . to the end of the earth" (Acts 1:8). Ten days after that came Pentecost and their baptism with the Holy Spirit, which Jesus had said the Father promised them.

As the days went by, the apostles began to learn how complete the changeover was. There really was a new order, the Spirit directing the new church as Jesus had directed the twelve. Jesus had sent the apostles, and later the seventy-two disciples, to carry his message. But now it is the Holy Spirit who says, "Set apart for me Barnabas and Saul for the work to which I have called them" (Acts 13:2).

It was the Holy Spirit who told Peter to go to the house of the gentile Cornelius; it was in response to the Holy Spirit that Peter baptized him and other uncircumcised men (Acts 10–11). Even after this, the question of whether gentiles who became Christians were obliged to observe Mosaic rituals—circumcision, especially—continued to trouble minds, Peter's included. A council of apostles and presbyters, attended by Paul and Barnabas, thrashed the matter out (Acts 15). We don't have all the details, but we notice that there is no mention of anything Jesus had said or done about gentiles while he was on earth. The decision in favor of freedom was expressed as, "It has seemed good to the Holy Spirit and to us" (verse 28).

In slighter matters also we find the Holy Spirit in operation. It was "through the Spirit" that Agabus prophesied that there was to be a great famine, so that it was decided to send relief to "the brethren who lived in Judea" (Acts 11:28-29). When the Ethiopian eunuch was driving along the Gaza road, it was the Spirit who said to Philip the deacon, "Go up and join this chariot"—and Philip instructed the eunuch in the Christian faith and baptized him; after which "the Spirit of the Lord" carried Philip away (8:29, 39).

Throughout Acts, Jesus gives no directives to any except Paul—once on the Damascus road and once in a vision at night (23:11). Paul needed the personal sending by Jesus if he was to rank with the other apostles. Even so, Jesus gives him his mission only in the most general terms; the Spirit will attend to the details. For example, it is the Spirit who orders him not to go into Bethynia.

The daily conduct of the church and of the individual Christian is the affair of the Holy Spirit. So it was as Christ established it. So it is and will be to the end of life on earth. We might ask ourselves whether our own interest in the Spirit is as great as his primacy in our lives demands.

In the days when Catholics talked about their religion more than most of us now do, one heard some such phrase as "the poor Holy Ghost, we neglect him so." Poor? Deprived of our interest in him, he had to make out as best he could with the company of the Father and the Son. There was indeed impoverishment in that neglect, but it was not his.

For our present purpose, we may wonder what compensation the apostles found in the promise that the Holy Spirit would replace the Jesus they had come to know and love. How much had they realized of what Jesus was saying? How much, in fact, did the Holy Spirit mean to them at that moment?

Who or what did they think Jesus was sending to take his place? Jesus was someone; the Spirit could hardly be that—a divine influence, perhaps. But Jesus said, "When the spirit of truth is come"—*someone,* therefore, not just something. But who? What? Learned men like Nicodemus and Joseph of Arimathea, perhaps even some of the apostles, would often have seen "the Spirit of God" in the Old Testament. They would have seen the phrase as a way of speaking of God himself, God in action, just as "the Word of God" was God in utterance. But even the Messiah could hardly send *God* as a substitute! The questions they must have asked themselves we too must answer. It can be profitable to study what was there for the apostles *before* Jesus gave the phrase "the Spirit" so surprising a turn.

PART I

Who Is the Spirit?

ONE
In the Beginning

What did "the Spirit" mean to the eleven men gathered round Jesus at the supper table? In the Bible, they knew, there is repeated mention of "the Spirit of God," which, as we have seen, meant God in operation, God acting upon the world and mankind. Thus what Spirit means is an outflow of whatever God means. What does the Old Testament tell of God himself?

We can examine the thirty-nine books of the Hebrew Bible, plus the extra seven that the Jews of Egypt included in the Greek translation of the Bible they had made a century before Christ. Of what the learned made of these half-million words we have a fair idea, for many of their commentaries still exist. Of what the eleven made of it, as it entered into their religion as they actually practiced it, we cannot know. It probably meant more to some of them than to others.

For ourselves, not Scripture scholars, much is to be learned about our special topic from the first chapter of the Bible's first book. For the Spirit of God meets us in its first verse.

Around the year 900 B.C., three hundred years after the Jews had come out of slavery in Egypt, King Solomon was reigning in Jerusalem. His scholars collected and arranged the stories that had come down through the centuries. The collection opened with the book called Genesis, or rather with its second chapter on how mankind began.

The first chapter was added five hundred years later as an introduction to a new and enlarged edition of the whole work. It is a kind of psalm, hymning the creation of the universe. It is astounding how much the writer managed to tell of God in the psalm's few hundred words.

God was one, as against the polytheisms of Egypt and Mesopotamia and Syria. He was the creator of all things whatsoever. Among the things he created were the sun and the moon—created not at the beginning but on the fourth day, not as gods—which for countless millions they were—but as conveniences for men and women. God created by his word. He said, "Let there be light." He said, "Let the waters bring forth swarms of living creatures"—and so it happened. God, then, was a person, "someone" not "something," "he" not "it"—this against the impersonal supreme being of so many religions to the East. In vast distinction from the deities of the pagans, who strike us as sexual maniacs, Israel's God had no consort—sex was his gift to plants, animals, men and women. Men and women he created in his own image and likeness. He asked for sacrifice, but not the human sacrifices practiced so appallingly by the pagans.

None of this was the invention of the writer of our first chapter. Indeed, in essence the whole chapter might have been a meditation on the "I am" that God had told Moses was his name—"Say this to the people of Israel, 'I AM has sent me to you'" (Exodus 3:14).

Our writer found the rest in the books of Moses, in the historical books, the psalms, and the prophetical writings; most of this was already there for him (and us) to read. Scripture contained much else, of course—about the good or ill use that man made of God's gifts; about God's choice of one nation (in whom all nations would be blessed) to proclaim his uniqueness; about his holiness and his majesty; about his love (Isaiah compared it to the love of a mother, 49:15); about our obedience and about the love he wants from us; about the union of love and obedience that make the fullness of life, the union we meet long after in Christ's words, "If you love me, keep my commandments."

This was the God who had created all things by his word, who breathed and man became a living spirit. When Jesus said to the five-husbanded woman at the well in Samaria, "God is spirit," he was using a phrase that happens not to be in the Old Testament. Could it have been? The Hebrew writers constantly use the word "spirit," which, as we shall see, is the Hebrew word *ruah* (or *ruach*)—wind.

"Wind" was a good metaphor or simile for God. God was unseen and powerful; so was the wind. It is the least material of all created things, the least earthy of the things of earth. *Ruah* settled into its highest use as "spirit" in our sense, a term used of men and angels and God.

But as to what God actually is, the Hebrew mind does not seem to have concerned itself very much. Their interest was in what he had done for them and what he demanded of them, not on the "self" who had done the deeds and made the demands. There was so much richness in their day-to-day awareness of him; his presence, though it was unseen, was so continuously with them that the question "*what* he is" no more occurred to them than the question "*whether* he is." One wonders how many of them had ever met a hard-shell atheist. "Spirit" was a satisfying metaphor, but like many a devout Christian, the Hebrews used it constantly without bothering about what depths might be in it.

Yet once we have heard Christ say, "God is spirit, and those who worship him must worship in spirit and in truth" (John 4:23), we have to make the choice. We must either clear our minds as to what spirit is, or we must struggle along without understanding a key word in our religion. If we do not give our minds to what Christ is saying, he might as well not have spoken. Given that God is spirit and our soul is spirit, not to have grasped the meaning of spirit could make our religion little more than a halfhearted approach to a dimly realized God. God's being merciful, that might be sufficient in peaceful times with nothing threatening; but in a world with chaos on the doorstep it is pathetic. Certainly we cannot go on to write about the Holy Spirit without a close look at the word "spirit."

What Is Spirit?

I have told the story so often that I am weary of it myself; but it was a milestone in my own religious thinking, and it might be so for others. I had used the word "spirit" in a lecture and a questioner said, "What is a spirit?" I answered—a spirit has no shape, no size, no dimensions, does not occupy space. The questioner said, "That's the best definition of nothing I've ever heard." He shook me, all right. I had told him what a spirit isn't and doesn't, with no word about what it is and does.

What does spirit do in us? It knows and loves and decides. A myriad of activities flow from those three, activities beyond the power of matter—general ideas, ideals and ideologies, mathematical and philosophical systems, moral convictions, the splitting of the atom, voyaging in outer space. In all these activities, mind and matter (including the matter of man's own body) are involved, but there is no question which uses which.

Still we have not got at what spirit *is*. What is it? Prepare to be reminded of an old-time classroom lecture you had happily forgotten. Spirit is the being that has no parts. Whenever the church uses the word "spirit," that is what she is saying. By "a part," she means any element in a being that is not the whole of it.

In a spirit—God, our soul—there is no division of parts as in matter. Therefore there is no dispersion of powers, but total concentration of being and of powers in one single act of being. The body has parts, each with its own function, which only it can perform. But all the things the soul does are done by the whole soul, for there is no element in the soul that is not the whole of it. It knows, loves, hates, wants, chooses, refuses to choose, decides, animates a body. And one single soul does each of these things with the whole of itself.

Two things emerge from spirit's absence of parts—it does not occupy space; it is everlasting.

Space is emptiness. A being that has parts can spread them in it! Even the minutest material thing has parts—the top is not the bottom, one end is not the other. But this is not so of the soul, not so of God: They have no parts to spread. They are not in space.

What of permanence? A being with parts can be taken apart; therefore it can always become something else by union with parts taken from some other source. But a spirit, having no parts, cannot be taken apart; it has no parts to be taken from it. It is the whole of itself. One can conceive of God's annihilating it—the being who alone can make something of nothing could reduce something to nothing. But God speaks only of two ends to earthly life—eternal happiness or eternal loss—no third. "It is appointed for men to die once," says Scripture, "and after that comes judgment" (Hebrews 9:27).

Space is so much a part of our mental habit that to speak of a being existing without occupying space seems like a flat contradiction in terms—a definition of nothing, in fact! We remember perhaps how long the problem held Augustine back, superb as his mind was. But if we ask ourselves what the terms are in which we feel contradiction, we might find it hard to state them. Division of parts is necessary if a being is to occupy space, but why should dividedness be necessary for existence?

The Spirit in Creation

Reading Genesis, we might think we are being given two accounts of the creation, contradictory accounts at that. If we do we are reading carelessly. The second chapter is about mankind's beginning in the universe; it is telling a story. The first chapter, added later as we have seen, is about the beginning of the universe itself. It is not telling a story but hymning a glory. The writer of the first had the second chapter before him. If he puts the making of man after the appearance of vegetation instead of before, he clearly thinks the order of creation a matter of no vital importance—not what his psalm is about.

Given the subject of our present book, it is worth noting that the account of creation in chapter 1 begins with the Spirit of God "moving over the face of the waters." There are those who translate the Hebrew word "spirit" (*ruah*) as a common noun meaning "wind," and the phrase "of God" as "mighty." Both translations, "Spirit of God" and "mighty wind," are grammatically possible. *Ruah* appears variously in Scripture, both in its primary meaning of air in motion—as wind, as the breath of man's mouth—but also as spirit in its richest meaning in man and angels and God.

But in that first chapter, *ruah* is translated "God"

forty times. God's action is what the hymn is about. It would be strange if in its first appearance it did *not* mean God. Only a raw beginner at writing could be as clumsy as that, and there was nothing raw about this writer. A raw writer might have thought it interesting to tell of the weather, but the information would have no particular point in it, whereas the Spirit of God moving over the waters has a world of meaning.

The actual creation is shown as God speaking, saying, uttering a word. "God said, 'Let there be light,' and there was light," and on to "'Let us make man in our image. . . .' So God created man in his own image; . . . male and female he created them." Psalm 33 phrases this, "By the word of the LORD the heavens were made, and all their host by the breath of his mouth" (33:6).

From end to end of Scripture we have this alternation of "spirit" and "word." To the men of the Old Testament, the Trinity had not been shown. They were not to know that the word was to be made flesh in Christ, that the Word was a divine person—God the Son. They were not to know that the Son would reveal that the Spirit too was a divine person. The Old Testament tells of the movement upward toward the incarnation, from the first level of religious understanding to the hour when mankind was ready for the fullness of revelation in Christ.

Newman has said that truth can be error to minds unprepared for it. To have told of the Trinity too early would all too easily have meant three gods, three idols, three altars.

It may be of interest later to remember that the Hebrew verb for the Spirit *moving* over the water would have been used for a bird hovering over its nest. I have read somewhere that some of the Jewish scholars would call the bird a dove. But in the temple ritual as it developed, the dove was the sacrifice of the poor—carpenters and their wives, for instance.

TWO

The Son of God

We may now return to the eleven apostles eating their last meal with Jesus before Calvary and hearing him say that it was better for them that he go away *because* otherwise the Holy Spirit would not come. They were near the end of their training period. In a few weeks, they would see Jesus rising into the sky till a cloud hid him from their gaze.

It is not likely that the promise of the Spirit at this eleventh hour shed much light for them or brought much comfort. It may indeed have seemed just one more puzzle to add to the strangeness of the world in which they had lived this last couple of years with Jesus. After all, how much had they grasped about the Carpenter himself? What was he? Who was he? Unless they believed in him, they would not accept his statement about a spirit who was to lead them into all truth. Nor should we.

The Baptist had spoken of Jesus as one mightier than himself. None of the apostles would have had any difficulty in believing this, not John and Andrew certainly, who had been the Baptist's disciples and had left him to follow the Carpenter. That Jesus was in fact mightier they could readily believe, if only because of the miracles beyond counting that they had seen him work—the Baptist had not raised the dead, had not turned water into wine, had in fact worked no miracles at all. The poet Keats was not thinking of miracles when he said, "Things seen are mightier than things heard," but he might well have been; and the "things heard" from Jesus had gone far beyond the Baptist's simpler message. Indeed, the miracles happening before their eyes must have been less of a strain on their minds than so many of the things he said, especially the shorter ones like "He who loves father or mother more than me is not worthy of me" (Matthew 10:37). If that were not true, then it was megalomania. But what if it were true?

All this—such a phantasmagoria of incredible words and deeds—the apostles must many a time have talked about among themselves far into the night. There is something farcical about the only such conversation of which we are told. They were arguing about which of them should have the highest place in the kingdom the Carpenter was to found (Mark 9:34). If only doubting Thomas had written a gospel. But Thomas was a couple of centuries dead when the so-called gospel of Thomas was written.

By the time of the Last Supper they could not doubt that Jesus was more than human. There was the Sermon on the Mount with its incredible "Think not that I have come to abolish the law and the prophets"—as if a young man today were to tell a vast crowd in New York's Central Park that he did not mean to abolish the presidency or tear up the Constitution. The normal reaction would be a derisive "Who does he think he is?" Soon the cousins of Jesus would be calling him mad and wanting to put him under restraint—a not-unknown reaction in families with an exceptional member. But for derision we must wait for the high priest's palace, and Herod's court, and Calvary.

To Jews, what Jesus went on to say in the Sermon on the Mount must have sounded like naked blasphemy. Half a dozen times he used the formula, "You have heard that it was said to the men of old. . . . But I say to you." By whom had the things he chose for comment been said of old? By God himself, on Mount Sinai, giving the Ten Commandments to Moses.

So who was he? Who could he be? Man-plus, evidently. But what could this particular plus mean? Could a man, with whatever new and unprecedented powers, say some of the things he was saying? Elijah could not have said them; Moses could not. Consider a handful of statements from the gospels:

"Your sins are forgiven" (Mark 2:5).
"The Son of man is lord of the
sabbath" (Matthew 12:8).
"The sabbath was made for man, not
man for the sabbath" (Mark 2:27).
"Before Abraham was, I am" (John 8:58).
"He who eats my flesh and drinks my
blood has eternal life, and I will raise him
up at the last day" (John 6:54).

At this last one, many of them left him, and he made
no effort to soften or explain away what he had said.
To the twelve he said, "Do you also wish to go away?"
Peter answered for them: "Lord, to whom shall we
go? You have the words of eternal life; and we have
believed, and have come to know, that you are the
Holy One of God" (John 6:67-69).

Jesus said and did things that make sense (if sense
be the word) only as coming from one who was divine.
Which was he, human or divine? Could he be both?
That would hardly have occurred to any of them.

The phrase "son of man," which he, and he alone,
used for himself told nothing except that there was
something to tell. It simply means "man"—God had
used it a good hundred times in addressing the prophet
Ezekiel.

Why did he not simply tell them who he was, what he was, and go on from there? Why, as many a street-corner heckler has asked, didn't he put his cards on the table? There are two overwhelming reasons why that would have been impossible.

The first is that Jews of that day had an awareness of the majesty of God that might surprise many a devout Christian. If Jesus had simply asserted that he was God, they would have slain him in the moment of utterance. True, he had come in order to die; but it must be in his own time. The second is that people who did not know of the three persons in God would not even have known what he was saying. They would have slain him without ever finding out!

Slowly the apostles were seeing that there was something in him too large for human nature to contain. He clearly had human nature, but he overlapped it! It was Peter who (as we read in Matthew 16:16) made the breakthrough. In answer to Christ's challenge, "Who do you say that I am?" he said, "You are the Christ, the Son of the living God."

Jews of a special piety or holding special offices had been called "sons of God" in the Old Testament. That Peter meant far more than that is clear, as we are shown twice over. First there is Christ's reception of Peter's words, "Blessed are you, Simon Bar-Jona! For flesh and blood has not revealed this to you, but my Father who is in heaven" (Matthew 16:17); then there is the use the high priest made of them (brought to him by an informer perhaps) to open his cross-examination of Jesus (26:63).

Jesus now had to tell more, at least to the men he was training to bring him and his message to the world. But before he told it in words, he gave one more evidence of the uniqueness of his relationship with the Father. The transfiguration is given to us by all the Evangelists except John, and there is a general feeling that Luke's account is from John. Here is Matthew's:

> Jesus took with him Peter and James and John his brother, and led them up a high mountain apart. And he was transfigured before them, and his face shone like the sun, and his garments became white as light. And behold, there appeared to them Moses and Elijah, talking with him. . . . A bright cloud overshadowed them, and a voice from the cloud said, "This is my beloved Son, with whom I am well pleased; listen to him." (17:1-3, 5)

The three fell on their faces; when they raised their eyes, they saw no one but Jesus.

To the men close to Jesus he did at last disclose the secret: it is in Luke 9 that we hear it first. The transfiguration had happened, Luke tells us, and "he set his face to go to Jerusalem," where Calvary awaited him (Luke 9:51). Ahead he sent seventy-two disciples in pairs to heal the sick in his name, and to announce that the kingdom of God was at hand. On their return to him, they made their report. It sent him into a kind of ecstasy (10:21). For this is the only time we hear that he rejoiced—"rejoiced in the Holy Spirit," rejoiced because the Father had shown to these nobodies-in-particular, these "babes" as he called them, things many a prophet and many a king had longed to see and hear.

It reads almost as if excitement wrenched the great secret from him: "All things have been delivered to me by my Father; and no one knows who the Son is except the Father, or who the Father is except the Son and any one to whom the Son chooses to reveal him" (Luke 10:22).

Reading the words now, with nineteen centuries of meditation and argument back and forth, we may feel that this is decisive. There is the unparalleled statement of a mutual interknowledge between Father and Son, with nothing to qualify or modify it. It is hard not to read it as an equality in being, all summed up in the phrase "All things have been delivered to me by my Father." The Father is the source. The Son holds all as received from him; but what he has received is all. That is the essence of the mystery.

In the light of those earlier things that the apostles—and we—have heard him say, at least the assertion of divinity would be hard to miss.

As to the further depths in Christ's own words, Peter knew more when, in his second speech after Pentecost, he told the crowd, "You killed the author of life." And Thomas knew more when he addressed the risen Christ as "my Lord and my God." So did John, many years later still, when he opened his gospel with, "In the beginning was the Word, and the Word was with God, and the Word was God. . . . And the Word became flesh and dwelt among us" (John 1:1, 14).

At any rate, by the time they heard Jesus say he would send the Holy Spirit to take his place, the apostles did know of a duality within the Godhead—two selves, Father and Son. By the time the Last Supper ended, they got the first suggestion of a third.

THREE
The Third Person

John begins his long account of the Last Supper (chapters 13–17): "Before the feast of the Passover, when Jesus knew that his hour had come to depart out of this world to the Father, having loved his own who were in the world, he loved them to the end." At the supper he told these men he loved that he must leave them.

The apostles were not tongue-tied, not in the least afraid to question Jesus. When he said that they could not yet come where he was going but that they would follow him there "afterward," Peter asked, "Lord, where are you going?" and Thomas asked, "How can we know the way?" When he spoke of his Father, Philip said, "Show us the Father, and we shall be satisfied." When he said that he would manifest himself to those who keep his commandments and love him, his cousin Jude asked, "How is it that you manifest yourself to us and not to the world?"—a question the cousinry had worked themselves up about earlier, as we read in John's seventh chapter.

But, as often, we feel that there were questions

clamoring to be asked and that there is no sign that the apostles asked them. When Jesus said, "I go to prepare a place for you, . . . that where I am you may be also" (John 14:2-3), we feel that we would have examined him closely about that place. When he said that it was better for them that he go because otherwise the Spirit would not come, we should like to hear them ask why the coming of the one involved the going of the other. Even when he said that the Spirit, the Paraclete, is to take his place when he leaves them (14:16), there is no question recorded from any of them.

Some of them, we remember, had been disciples of the Baptist and would have heard John speak of one who "will baptize you with the Holy Spirit and with fire" (Matthew 3:11). Was Jesus saying that something of this sort would happen when he left them? John's phrase was splendid indeed, but it did not cast a great deal of light on what the experience would be; every word seemed to call for explanation. And this coming of the Spirit—would it be something like the coming of the dove on Jesus himself at his baptism? Some of them may have heard the Baptist say that the dove was the Spirit, but what light could a dove cast upon the Spirit of God?

They knew that the Spirit had worked in and through Jesus. They had heard Jesus say that it is by the Spirit that he casts out devils (Matthew 12:28), and indeed they themselves had exercised power over demons in his name (Luke 10:17). But this promised coming of the Spirit when Jesus was no longer with them seemed to call for more knowledge about who and what the Spirit may be than they had yet been given.

At the Last Supper, Jesus began to open his mind to them on this Spirit whose coming was to compensate for his own leaving:

> I will ask the Father and he will give you another Paraclete that he may abide with you for ever, the Spirit of Truth whom the world cannot receive because it neither sees him nor knows him; you know him because he shall abide [remain] with you and shall be in you. (John 14:16-17, Douay-Rheims Version)

There are three words here for which the apostles, and better scholars than the apostles, were not prepared—"Paraclete," "another," "abide."

Paraclete is really new—the very word is new, found nowhere else in Greek. It is a noun derived from the verb *para-kalein—para,* meaning "alongside;" *kalein,* meaning "to summon." The whole verb means to summon to one's side, to call to one's aid, especially as an advocate either pleading one's cause or defending one against an enemy, or even as a comforter in one's affliction.

Another Paraclete. Jesus, leaving them, will send *another* paraclete in his place. In John's first epistle (1 John 2:1), Jesus is actually called so—"If any one does sin, we have an advocate [paraclete] with the Father, Jesus Christ the righteous." By its very strangeness the word Paraclete catches the eye.

But "*abide*" is both new in what it means and vastly important. In the Old Testament, the Spirit could aid or enlighten or rebuke. But to act upon men from within, to *remain* with them permanently—with this we have "indwelling" and practically a definition of sanctifying grace.

As Jesus speaks on, there is further light: "The Paraclete, the Holy Spirit, whom the Father will send in my name, he will teach you all things, and bring all things to your mind, whatever I shall have said to you" (John 14:26, DRV).

As the words came from the Lord's mouth the apostles may not have caught the significance of the word "he." "*He* will teach you all things." "He" occurs a dozen times in the discourse, all the more surprising because the word for "spirit," *pneuma,* is neuter. So the Spirit is a person: "someone" not "something." Jesus who was someone was to be replaced not by a divine action or attribute or by a divine influence, but by another *someone*. Jesus, the first Paraclete, was divine. Was the second?

It would be difficult to be certain from the four gospels that he was divine. Only close to the end of Matthew do we find "Father, Son, and Holy Spirit"—in the formula for baptism. That was written perhaps forty years later; but baptism had been going on all the forty years from the day of Pentecost, and indeed the new Christians had been uttering God in three terms from much earlier.

That considerable scholar, the Jesuit Karl Rahner, finds forty such triads, groupings of three, in the New Testament. In the earliest Christian writing that has reached us—Paul's first letter to the Thessalonians, written within twenty years after Christ's death—we find "Pray constantly, give thanks in all circumstances; for this is the will of God in Christ Jesus for you. Do not quench the Spirit" (5:17-19).

The second letter to the Corinthians, written not long after, ends, "The grace of the Lord Jesus Christ and the love of God and the fellowship of the Holy Spirit be with you all" (13:14). The names vary. The first of the three is sometimes called "Son," sometimes

"Lord"; the second may be either "God" or "Father"; the third is always "Spirit." If the Spirit is not divine as the Father and Son are, it is strange to find him so regularly there, as if he were one who does not really belong but cannot be left out! At the end of Matthew's gospel, we read how Jesus instructs the apostles: "Go therefore and make disciples of all nations, baptizing them in the name [the Greek means "into the name"] of the Father and of the Son and of the Holy Spirit" (Matthew 28:19). It is the only time Scripture has that precise wording, to Christians the best known. And for a reader of Scripture , the word *name* in the singular is decisive—if the third member of the group shares the name, he shares the nature. If the first two are divine, so is the third.

One further look at a question we feel we should have asked had we been at the Last Supper: Why was it better for the apostles, and thus for us, that Jesus should go? If they had asked it, then we should not need to ask it now.

We get light on the answer only by looking at what followed Jesus' death and resurrection and ascension. In the opening statement of John's account of the supper there is a phrase that may be rather surprising if we are giving our minds to every word: "When Jesus knew that his hour had come *to depart out of this world to the Father"* (John 13:1). So his going to his Father was not just a happy ending to his redemptive agony—it was his hour, the climax, redemption achieved.

Made perfect by his sufferings (Hebrews 5:8-9), Jesus is the head of redeemed humanity. As such he is taken by God to himself. It is Christ Jesus, Paul tells us, "who was raised from the dead, who is at the right hand of God, who indeed intercedes for us" (Romans 8:34). Of this interceding we read in Hebrews 7:24-25 that Jesus "holds his priesthood permanently, because he continues for ever. Consequently he is able for all time to save those who draw near to God through him, since he always lives to make intercession for them."

His intercession is the offering of himself—once slain, now forever living—to his Father. That offering is to continue till all who are to be saved have reached the goal. That is the new order in which the Holy Spirit now functions in the church and in each one of us. In Christ's presenting himself before the throne of God, he's our salvation.

All that this means for us we cannot know till we too have reached the place he has gone to prepare for us (John 14:2). The New Testament writers grow toward ecstasy as they write of it: "We see Jesus, who for a little while was made lower than the angels, crowned with glory and honor because of the suffering of death, so that by the grace of God he might taste death for every one" (Hebrews 2:9).

FOUR

Father, Son, and Holy Spirit

If a reader does not find in Scripture the threefold personality of God, he or she might still learn much from Scripture about what the Holy Spirit can do in us and for us; but who he is, what he is, and why he comes into the picture at all would have to remain a blank. It would be unthinkable for any Christian to ask if that would really matter, unthinkable to say that, provided we get whatever gifts the Spirit may have to give us, who or what he is need not concern us. No, one could not actually say that, not in so many words, but it would be possible to act as if it did not matter.

It seems ridiculous to try to give a skeleton analysis of Father, Son, and Holy Spirit, the reality without which there is no reality. Yet Christ has given us lights upon the inner life of God; he did not intend this to be ignored. At least we can make a beginning; in all eternity we shall not have made an end. For more than nineteen centuries the church has lived Jesus' teaching on the three-in-one and applied her mind to it. There is light and delight in applying ours.

The Word Was God

Within the proportions of this book, we can make as good a beginning as any with the opening of the fourth gospel: "In the beginning was the Word, and the Word was with God, and the Word was God." It is not difficult to understand what Jesus was saying, so clear a development is it of "no one knows the Son but the Father and no one knows the Father but the Son." But to take the words in and make them one's own—life will never be the same after.

God utters a word. He does not utter a word as we utter it, with air from the lungs, shaped by tongue and teeth and lips, sounding in the ears. God is a spirit with no such bodily structuring. His word can only be soundless, within himself, a mental word, therefore, akin to a concept or idea.

The Word was with God. The concept, the idea, did not pass away in the utterance; it remains with God, it belongs. That is difficult enough perhaps. But the Word *was* God! What mental word, what idea, could possibly be God?

Inside the church and out, minds have wrestled with that question endlessly; a mass of theological thinking has flowered from it. I give what we may call the mainstream of that flow—the Catholic doctrine as given by

Rome and by the great churches of the East, accepted by Martin Luther in outline, and by John Calvin. The one idea that could possibly *be* God is his idea of himself. This answer is mysterious enough, but what other answer would be even worth bothering to reject?

God, then, knowing himself with total knowing-power, produces an idea of himself.

Realize that we have only the words of human language at our disposal. They were produced and continually developed by the human race in order to express not the reality of God, but only what of reality we have experienced by our senses and the instruments that extend their range, by our intelligence and our will and our emotions and our imagination, our dreams, our mystical moments. This is a vast area, but the God who willed our existence out of nothing lies beyond it.

We cannot know him as he knows himself! Our thoughts about him and their utterance in word and gesture must always fall short of his reality.

Still, even at their crudest, there is light and nourishment in our thoughts and words. From the beginning, God has wanted to be known by us. It is part of the uniqueness of the Judeo-Christian religion that he wants not only to be known but loved by human beings. Why else would he have made them in his own image and likeness?

We use human language in our speaking to God. He uses it in his speaking to us. And genuine communication it is.

The idea of himself that God conceives, the concept he forms, is of course totally adequate. Pause upon this. You have an idea of yourself—I too and all of us—but at best it is a sketchy idea. It is not the whole you—too much left out, a lot of illusion woven into it. How far it falls short you keep on discovering—when a friend tells you what he thinks of you, for instance, or when you do something that reveals elements in you that you hadn't suspected. The plain truth is that we do not know ourselves very well. When a stranger says, "Tell me about yourself," we can babble about things we have done or experienced, people we are related to. But if we tried to tell the stranger about the self that did, or experienced, or has the important relatives, the babble would trickle into silence. No, we do not know very well the beings we are.

But God's self-knowledge is perfect. The idea in which he utters this perfect knowledge is equally perfect. There is nothing that is true of himself that is not a living truth in his self-idea. It is eternal, all knowing, all loving—as he is. His self-idea is a person as he is, a self as he is, God as he is.

Thus, within the one Godhead, the one divine reality, there are two selves. Thinking outward from John's "Word," *logos* in Greek, we have been seeing them as the knower and his idea of himself. But after the first dozen or so verses, "Word" disappears from John's gospel. For the rest of it, and always from Christ himself, we find the word "Son." The Father produces this second person not for knowledge, but for companionship.

We might wonder why John uses "Word" in the gospel at all, since he ceases using it so soon. Clearly both "idea-conceived" and "son-generated" represent the same relation of likeness. A son is of the same nature as his father; an idea is meant to express the object as it truly is. It is pleasant to realize that to express the production of the Second Person, two words of human procreation—"conceive" and "generate"—are called into service.

When it is of God we are talking, "the idea" has one not-small advantage over "the Son." We might well wonder how a spirit could generate a son; with the divine mind conceiving the perfect self-idea, that particular difficulty is not thrust at us.

The Spirit Is Breathed

Is there an explanation of the Third Person as spirit to match the *generating* of the Son, the *uttering* of the word? "Son" and "word" both suggest the way of his production as a person. Does "spirit" throw equal light on the production of the Third?

In fact, "spirit" seems to raise one instant problem. Given that God is a spirit, why should the third possessor of the divine nature be given as specially his own a name that applies equally to the first and second? This question is not just playing with words: there is light at the end of the game.

To St. Augustine we owe the insight that, as the Second Person is produced within the divine nature by knowledge, the Third is produced by way of love. Knowledge and love, the highest activities of created spirits, thus reach their own supreme height in the uncreated.

The utterance of love within the lover is not as easy for us to put into words as the utterance within the knower of the act of knowing. For this latter we have the words "idea" and "mental word." But for love, what is there? In what does love utter itself best? It must be something proceeding immediately from the organism, proceeding so immediately from it that it remains within it. Our Lord's term is "Spirit"-breath. The Fathers of the Church have used a variety of terms.

The Holy Spirit is, for instance, the "sigh" of Father and Son. The term is perhaps not wholly satisfying, for transience seems the very essence of a sigh. One can conceive (though not, of course, imagine) eternal ecstasy uttered in an eternal sigh. Yet again, one associates a certain discouragement with a sigh. A song is better, a song in the heart. Another term the church fathers like is "kiss"; but it is not easy to think of a kiss as a person. And while, in the world the Fathers knew, the kiss was a universal way of expressing love, it is not so in the vaster world that the explorers were to open up in the centuries to follow. St. Augustine uses the word *donum*, gift. This suggests what the Holy Spirit does, or is, to us, but not so readily what he is to Father and Son. We find the word *vinculum* (bond) used, as though the Third Person were a bond linking the First and Second, but we must not forget the bond that already exists between thinker and thought.

I hope readers will not mind that the last two paragraphs are from my earlier book, *God and the Human Condition* (vol. 1, p. 225). I tried to rewrite them but only made them worse.

"Sigh" and "song" and "kiss," like "gift" and "bond," carry a hint of the immense activity, the immense productiveness, that Scripture shows pouring out of the Holy Spirit. Obviously, "spirit" is best. Otherwise the Third Person would not have been called "Spirit" in both the Old and New Testaments.

"Spirit," as used of God, is the lifting of a simpler, cruder word into a higher meaning. *Spiritus* in Latin, *pneuma* in Greek, *ruah* in Hebrew—one way or other all these words can stand for air in motion, wind blowing, lungs breathing. Our ancestors saw air—invisible, essential to life, powerful—as the material element best suited to be used of the unseen, life-giving, omnipotent God. But it is in the basic meaning of "breath" that "spirit" is used of the Third Person. The Son is generated; the Spirit is *breathed*.

But what can "breath" tell of the production of the Third Person, as "generated" tells of the Second? It would be sad to have light on the production of the Son, and not of the Spirit.

The connection of breath with life hardly needs emphasis—the most primitive people are aware that when breath stops, the man is dead. We are born again, says our Lord, of water and the Holy Spirit. Supernatural life, like natural life, begins with breathing.

Has breath any similar connection with love? Not obviously perhaps. But there is a connection: love has an effect on the breathing, if only because it can make the heart beat quicker! Perhaps one is being fanciful.

I do not suggest that we know the whole story behind the Spirit's name. God may have a reason of his own for putting the name "Spirit" into our heads—in the very first verses of Scripture's very first book.

From the Father and the Son

Let us return now to our idea of ourself. We may dislike it to the point of feeling suicidal. We may in a general way like it, rather pleased that it is as it is. We do not think of *it* as liking or disliking *us,* for our idea of ourself is only something, not someone. But God's idea of himself is someone.

Father and Son, thinker and thought, equally loving, can unite in an act of love, pouring into it all they have and are, filling the whole divine nature with lovingness. The whole of their nature is now expressed as love, a love divine as they are, eternal as they are—a third self within the one all-knowing, all-seeing, all-loving God-head. The Father, knowing himself totally, produces the Son, divine as *he* is; Father and Son, loving each other totally, produce the Spirit, divine as *they* are.

In the Nicene Creed, we say that we believe "in the Holy Spirit, the Lord, the giver of life, who proceeds from the Father and the Son." The word *filioque,* "from the Son," was added in the fourth century to answer a question then being asked about the relationship between Son and Spirit. The Eastern Orthodox have not accepted this addition—for them, the Spirit proceeds from the Father only. Feeling runs strong. If only Augustine could have been at the Council of Ephesus, which declared Our Lady *Theotokos,* Mother of God. But he died in 430, the year before the council opened.

It has been suggested that to speak of the Spirit as "proceeding from the Father *through the Son*" (the phrase has been used before, not successfully) might be acceptable to both sides. It is not for me to say whether either would accept this. But in the purely logical order, it would seem that a thought living in the mind of the thinker could hardly be excluded from any other activity of the thinker—his love, for instance. To summarize the doctrine: There are three who are God, but not three gods, only one God. Jesus who revealed the Trinity utters also God's unity—"The Lord our God, the Lord is one" (Mark 12:29).

The doctrine of the Trinity is mysterious, of course. But at least let us see what the mystery is not. Observe that all is within one being, outside whom it does not extend. The thought lives within the mind of the thinker. If, by an impossibility, the thinker ceases to think it, the thought (which the Son is) would cease to be. The love exists in the nature of the two who join to produce it. If, by an impossibility, they ceased to love, the lovingness between them (which the Spirit is) would cease to be. God exists as Father, Son, and Spirit; one life stream flows through all of them.

It is of the nature of the Father thus to know himself. It is of the nature of the Father and the Son thus to love. By the Spirit, as by the Son, all is received; but what is received is all.

FIVE
Some Clarifications

Language

I f we try to tell an unbeliever about the Trinity as
we have just been discussing it, we shall quite certainly be met with the word "anthropomorphism."
This means that human beings imagine a God of the
same sort as themselves but without their limitations;
humanity's God is simply a human being writ large.

There are indeed resemblances between ourselves
and our creator, but not because we have imagined
them. They exist simply because human beings were
made by their creator in his own image and likeness.
Given this we can use the likeness as a first step in the
study of the original.

Thus the church's reasoning from our likeness is not
an effort to prove that Father, Son, and Holy Spirit are
like this or like that. It is simply a God-aided effort to
fathom and make our own what he has revealed to us
about himself. He has made it clear that he wants to
be loved by us. Therefore he wants to be known by

us, since each new truth we learn about him is a new reason for loving him.

This brings us back to the insufficiency of human language. For instance, consider the term "three persons." Just as "spirit" started off as "wind," invisible and powerful, "person" comes from *persona*—Greek and Roman actors wore masks in plays, their voices sounding through their masks. *Persona* came to mean the character behind the mask, the person whose identity the mask indicated. For us, "person" has reached its full reality as one who is aware of himself as himself, who knows and loves.

The words "Father" and "Son" used of God are not of our invention. God himself has given them to us in Scripture, and for the Third Person he has given us "Spirit." But we must remind ourselves constantly that in God these words possess a reality beyond anything known to us. Angels, for instance, who do not procreate, would not think in terms of "Father" and "Son." Lacking lungs, they would not have the breathing apparatus that is at the base of the idea of "Spirit." It is to human beings that God has given these terms as the closest in our experience to their reality in him. It has been suggested—by whom, I do not remember, Augustine perhaps—that it might be truer to speak of *tres nescio quid*—three "I know not whats." But that would give us no light at all: "Father," "Son," and "Spirit" do give light.

"Holy" Spirit

Why, we may wonder, given the holiness of the First Person and the Second, is the Third called "holy?" Here again it is Scripture that writes his name so, three or four times in the Old Testament, scores of times in the New. It is not God's holiness that is credited to the Spirit, since it is not applied to the Father and the Son. It is ours: his special function is to bring us the gifts that lead us to holiness, beginning, we remember, with life itself, the life of grace in our souls. In the Nicene Creed, he is called *dominum et vivificantem,* Lord and lifegiver. Giving is his special concern. In Augustine's view, this is so because the Spirit subsists by the way of love—loving and giving go together.

God Is Love

If one does not believe in the threefold personality, what does one make of John's great statement, "God is love" (1 John 4:8)? Whom does a solitary God, a one-person God, love? He could love us, the human beings he has created, but that would be a thin substitute for love. We, in our finiteness, could not comprehend his love or return it. He would be eternally loving beneath himself! Men and women, in fact, have always been afraid of the solitary God. This may be one reason why the paganisms multiplied gods—the wrong reaction to a profoundly right instinct. Pagans had a feeling that it was not good for God to be alone! Within the Trinity there is no aloneness, but love is given infinitely and infinitely returned.

Eternity

Eternity is worth a longer look. Built as we are, we live moment-by-moment, not because our souls are like that, but because our bodies are. The body, though it is the lesser partner, tends to dominate the partnership. We do not possess our whole being at any moment. Something of our reality has drifted into the past—we are no longer all we were. Something too has not yet come to us—it is still in the future. It seems a pointless jesting to say that at no moment are we all there, but this is very much the point. By contrast, there is no moment at which God is not all there, wholly himself. That is what we mean by eternity—God eternally present, wholly.

Evidently his presence is very different from ours, which is the "split instant" between a past that no longer is and a future that is not yet. Our "now" is so very fleeting it does not even last while we say it. While we are pronouncing the "n," the "ow" is still in the future; by the time we are saying "ow," the "n" has gone forever. But God's "now" abides. In eternity it is always now.

We have no experience of such a now, no experience of an infinite that possesses its own totality timelessly. But even if the imagination cannot picture it, our mind can be aware of depths in it, and find nourishment as we begin to move toward those depths.

Our habit of seeing things as past, present, future (like our habit of seeing things in space) is always liable to distort our understanding of Father, Son, Spirit. Time will keep breaking in. In spite of our firmest resolutions, we find ourselves thinking of the Son as younger than the Father—so often we have seen the Trinity presented as an old man with a long beard, a young man with a short beard, and a dove with no beard. In the human race, fathers are older than their sons, because a certain amount of time must roll by before they are mature enough to beget children.

It would be foolishness to think that a certain amount of eternity must roll by before the First Person of the Godhead is sufficiently developed to beget a son. Eternity does not roll by; God lacks no maturity. Simply by being God, he knows himself infinitely and conceives the living idea that is the Son. Father and Son are coeternal. Nor did they need to grow into the love from which the Holy Spirit proceeds. Simply by being what he is, God exists as Father, Son, and Holy Spirit.

The Order of Production

A related and much commoner error, deceiving even the elect, is to regard the roles of producing and being produced as deciding the measure of greatness. For example, if the Son has a role in the production of the Spirit, there are those who feel that there must be some kind of inferiority in the Spirit. But even among ourselves, sons are not necessarily inferior to fathers. William Shakespeare is a greater poet than old John Shakespeare. Where the producer and the one produced are wholly timeless, the principle is even clearer. In the logical order, a being must be known before he is loved, but the love may be greater than the knowledge! Where there is eternal co-existence, the question should not even have arisen.

Is It Too Complicated?

Why, we may wonder, did God reveal these elements in his own nature, which, as we hear them uttered, seem to say so little to us? Isn't it all just too complicated? Why not just let us get on with being good?

A full answer to that would take another book. All I can do here is indicate what two of the chapters in such a book would be about.

First, those who have given their minds to the mysteries of God's nature do not find that they add to the complication. The universe is immeasurably complex already. "Mysteries" in religion are not truths of which we can know nothing but truths of which we cannot know everything. To repeat a phrase, "we cannot know the self-existent being as well as he knows himself. It is a triumph of his ingenuity that we know him at all." It is not possible for us to know God as well as he knows himself. But, aided by God, we can grow in knowledge of him, and the knowledge gained sheds light both on the universe and on our lives in it—that is, it reduces not only the world's meaninglessness but our own, for we cannot even know ourselves as well as God knows us.

Second, God wants to be known by us. Generations of men and women beyond our counting—saints among them—have lived and gone their way with no awareness of the threefold personality in which God's unity finds unity's sheerest fullness. That God-made-man chose to reveal the secret of God's inner life is the supreme proof of his love.

Love, not just philanthropy, of course, wants not only to know the beloved *but to be known*. That supreme proof of his love God has not withheld from us. Our Lord said, "Greater love has no man than this, that a man lay down his life for his friends" (John 15:13). As man, he laid his life down for us. As God, he laid his life open to us. It would be a grim failure of love in us simply to wonder why he should have bothered.

PART II

The Spirit in Action

SIX

We Are in the Hands
of the Spirit

Action upon mankind, individually and in community, is the special function of the Holy Spirit. Theology tells us that the distinction of persons—each knowing himself as himself and glorying in each of the others as other—is lived within the being of God. God's action upon the created universe, theologians say, is of the three acting as one.

But Scripture encourages us to regard certain of these outside divine actions as proper to one or the other—to appropriate them to, associate them especially with, Father or Son or Holy Spirit. Creation, the making of something where nothing was, is appropriated to the Father, who within the Trinity is the source of all. The ordering of creation, that it may be not a shapeless, meaningless mass, is appropriated to the Son, who subsists in the Godhead by the way of intellect.

So we have Paul saying of the Son, "He is the image of the invisible God, the first-born of all creation; for in him all things were created, in heaven and on earth, visible and invisible, whether thrones or dominions or principalities or authorities [these last four words all represent angels, about whom the Colossians had some strange ideas]—all things were created through him and for him . . . in him all things hold together" (Colossians 1:15-17).

Paul summarizes thus: "There is one God, the Father, from whom are all things and for whom we exist, and one Lord, Jesus Christ, through whom are all things and through whom we exist" (1 Corinthians 8:6).

Within the reality created by the Father through the Son, we are shown the Spirit as giver of the gifts by which creatures can live the fullness of life. The Spirit subsists within the Godhead by the way of love. We may think of the creation of our universe as by the Father, through the Word, unto Love.

Genesis opens with God making all things, with the spirit of God moving over the waters, with creation affected by God's word. The man who wrote this may not have known in their depth all the immensities of what he was saying; he could hardly have said them better if he had! The Holy Spirit, his coauthor so to speak, had his own reasons for wanting them said like that. God had never existed, except as Father, Son, and Spirit.

Yet we must walk warily here. We cannot spread God out on a surgeon's table for our inspection or lay him down on a psychiatrist's couch for our analysis. Was there some reason within the divine nature for these appropriations of activity to one or another? We have not been told. Though each of the three persons has the whole divine nature, there is a difference in their ways of having it. Does this difference reach further? We can speculate. But we can give our hearts and minds only to what he tells us of himself. Certainly we are not to think of the three persons as an original and two copies.

In briefest outline we may look again at what we saw at the beginning of Part I.

Man's desire to be a law to himself, to choose what he wanted as against what God saw as right for him, ruined the order of the first planning. The Son, the Word in the mind of God, *through* whom the order had been made, became man and made a new order beyond the power of any individual to wreck. The wrecking power is limited to each self. After the wrecking of the first order, still more after the establishing of the new order by Christ's death and resurrection and ascension, the Holy Spirit's function was and is to give the gifts of knowledge and will that will enable humanity to find its fulfillment and reach its goal. We are in the hands of the Spirit.

SEVEN
The Spirit in the
Old Testament

"In the Beginning"

The New Testament leaves us in no doubt of the necessity of knowing the Old. Christ says to the Jews, "You search the scriptures, because you think that in them you have eternal life; and it is they that bear witness to me" (John 5:39). Further on in the same chapter, we hear him say, "If you believed Moses, you would believe me, for he wrote of me" (verse 46).

At Emmaus we have him saying to the two disciples, "Was it not necessary that the Christ should suffer these things and enter into his glory?" Then, "beginning with Moses and all the prophets, he interpreted to them in the scriptures the things concerning himself" (Luke 24:26-27).

In Genesis 2:24 we read, "Therefore a man leaves his father and his mother and cleaves to his wife, and they become one flesh."

It is not made clear who actually said this—hardly Adam (what father or mother had he?). Perhaps (we may think) the writer of Genesis said it. But Christ himself says that God said it! "Have you not read that he who made them from the beginning made them male and female, and said, 'For this reason a man shall leave his father and mother and be joined to his wife, and the two shall become one'?" (Matthew 19:4-5).

Consider two statements made by Peter: "Brethren, the scripture had to be fulfilled, which the Holy Spirit spoke beforehand by the mouth of David" (Acts 1:16), and later, "The prophets who prophesied of the grace that was to be yours searched and inquired about this salvation [of your souls] . . . the Spirit of Christ within them . . . predicting the sufferings of Christ and the subsequent glory. It was revealed to them that they were serving not themselves but you, in the things which have now been announced to you by those who preached the good news to you through the Holy Spirit sent from heaven" (1 Peter 1:10-12).

Sent to Rome and awaiting trial before Caesar, Paul "expounded the matter to them from morning till evening, testifying to the kingdom of God and trying to convince them about Jesus both from the law of Moses and from the prophets" (Acts 28:23). He told them, "The Holy Spirit was right in saying to your fathers through Isaiah the prophet: . . . 'This people's heart has grown dull, and their ears are heavy of hearing, and their eyes they have closed; lest they should perceive with their eyes, and hear with their ears, and understand with their heart, and turn for me to heal them'" (28:25, 27).

Prophets and Priests

It is strange that after his moving on the face of the waters at the creation, we next meet the Spirit of God on rather improbable lips. Pharaoh, deciding to put Egypt in Joseph's charge, said, "Can we find such a man as this, in whom is the Spirit of God?" (Genesis 41:38). After Pharaoh we must wait for another non-Jew, Balaam, of whom most of us remember only that his ass spoke to him. "Balaam lifted up his eyes, and saw Israel encamping tribe by tribe. And the Spirit of God came upon him," and having come there to curse Israel he blessed it instead (Numbers 24:2). It is the first time we read of the Spirit of God as the source of a prophecy. (This did not prevent the Jews from slaying Balaam not long after.)

With Samuel, we come at last upon a genuine prophet receiving from God light for the guidance of God's people. It was he who anointed Saul to be Israel's first king, promising him that "the spirit of the LORD will come mightily upon you, and you . . . shall be turned into another man" (1 Samuel 10:6). The "other man" that Saul became was a very strange one, but the promise as it stands is for all of us: the Holy Spirit, if we let him, will turn any one of us into another person, less unlike Christ, less like our selves. Samuel's action in anointing first Saul and then David, upon both of whom "the spirit of God came with power," settled beyond all question that Israel's king was to be God's servant, that what mattered in Israel's history lay in its relationship with God.

But there was nothing automatic about the gift of the Spirit, no guarantee of permanence. The will of man is free, and the Spirit of God will not force it, indeed cannot force it, without the will ceasing to be a will, and the man ceasing to be a man. There is a mystery here; in eternity we may see it untangled. Then as now the grace of God was not a laborsaving device. Saul and David and you and I are still under the rule, "Pray as if all depends on God; work as if all depends on ourselves."

We may place Samuel somewhere about 1000 B.C. Until the disappearance of prophecy three centuries before the coming of the Baptist, the theme of themes with all the prophets—varying as the levels of fidelity varied—was the relationship of God's people to God, especially with respect to their fidelity or infidelity to the covenant God had made with Moses. With Amos, social justice is vividly, almost spectacularly, shown in its failure. With Micah, the Spirit of the Lord is shown in its bearing on the moral life—Israel's, and ours:

> But as for me, I am filled with power,
>   with the spirit of the Lord,
>   and with justice and might,
> to declare to Jacob his transgression
>   and to Israel his sin. . . .
> Its heads give judgment for a bribe,
>   its priests teach for hire,
>   its prophets divine for money.
> (Micah 3:8, 11)

Micah is a short book. It is good to read it as a preparation for the reading of Isaiah, whose opening chapters were being written at about the same time, say around 740 B.C. Scholars seem to agree that there are three "Isaiahs." The first wrote most of chapters 1–39. To the second, whose name is not known to us, we owe chapters 40–55, written when the exile in Babylon was nearing its end. These chapters tell of the "suffering servant"—especially chapter 53, which Christ quotes at the Last Supper as the foretelling of what is about to happen to him (Luke 22:37). From chapter 55 to the end, we are reading the oracles of two of Isaiah's followers; it is hard to think that he would have disowned them!

The scathing account Isaiah gives of the sins of his people reads like Micah. But he sees a cleansing time for Israel, "when the Lord shall have washed away the filth of the daughters of Zion and cleansed the bloodstains of Jerusalem from its midst by a spirit of judgment and by a spirit of burning" (Isaiah 4:4). For both uses of "spirit," the Hebrew word is *ruah*—breath. We remember that the Spirit of God calls for a response from us.

Much might be demanded of the Jews because they had been given much. But all of us—Jews and gentiles, believers and nonbelievers—have received more from God than we were entitled to, and may even, unknowingly, have made a response pleasing to God!

All this time, in Israel and among its enemies, "prophecy" was continuous. There were whole groups of soothsayers, ready to foretell, to bless or curse, at the command or inducement of the nearest king. Jeremiah would one day mock the prophets of his own day who took the line that since Israel was the people of God, God would protect them whatever their level of fidelity to the covenant. He calls their compliance "wind," *ruah* in its lowest meaning. We do not know enough to assay the proportion of genuineness among them. But Samuel was at the head of such a group!

Isaiah faced the condition into which so much of Israel had let itself sink. Yet he said that salvation would come when "the Spirit is poured upon us from on high, and the wilderness becomes a fruitful field. . . . Then justice will dwell in the wilderness, and righteousness abide in the fruitful field. And the effect of righteousness will be peace, and the result of righteousness, quietness and trust for ever" (Isaiah 32:15-17).

One would like to remain with Isaiah. Let us at least have one more quotation, a foretelling of Jesus:

> There shall come forth a shoot from the
>   stump of Jesse [David's father],
> and a branch shall grow out of his
>   roots.
> And the Spirit of the LORD shall rest upon
>   him,
>   the spirit of wisdom and understanding,
>   the spirit of counsel and might,
>   the spirit of knowledge and the fear of
>   the Lord (11:12).

Isaiah gives them as gifts of the Holy Spirit to the Christ. We recite them still, with piety added, as the Spirit's gifts to us.

Let us consider one last quotation, this time from the second Isaiah (40:13). In showing himself as creator without human aid, God cries his challenge: "Who has directed the Spirit of the LORD, or as his counselor has instructed him?"

Ezekiel is not always remembered as that extreme rarity—a priest who was a prophet. He is remembered rather because of the vision of the wheels with which his book opens, rather perhaps from hearing the Negro spiritual than from meeting it in the Bible. Yet we might not have noticed the continuous presence of the Spirit within the wheels: "And the Spirit lifted me up and brought me in the vision by the Spirit of God into Chaldea, to the exiles" (11:24).

From Ezekiel too we have God's promise of a new spirit: "I will sprinkle clean water upon you. . . . A new heart I will give you, and a new spirit I will put within you; and I will take out of your flesh the heart of stone and give you a heart of flesh. And I will put my spirit within you" (36:25-27).

For the most part, the prophets have been instructing Israel as a community. The more we know of what was happening to the community, both within it and at the hands of the other great powers, the better we can understand what lessons the prophets have for us individually. Even without that kind of detailed knowledge, the lessons for us are clear.

In addition there are instructions specifically for us as individuals. The psalms are a rich guidebook to what God expects of us. Psalm 51, for instance, gives the teachings we have just heard from the second Isaiah:

> Create in me a clean heart, O God,
>   and put a new and right spirit within me.
> Cast me not away from thy presence,
>   and take not thy holy Spirit from me.
> Restore to me the joy of thy salvation,
>   and uphold me with a willing spirit.
> (51:10-12)

God wants a willing, not a grudging, obedience. And the essence of God's guiding is that he knows us better than we know ourselves, even before we know ourselves:

> Even before a word is on my tongue,
>   lo, O LORD, thou knowest it altogether.
> Thou dost beset me behind and before,
>   and layest thy hand upon me.

Such knowledge is too wonderful for me;
  it is high, I cannot attain it.
Whither shall I go from thy Spirit?
  Or whither shall I flee from thy
    presence?
If I ascend to heaven, thou art there!
  If I make my bed in Sheol, thou art
    there!
If I take the wings of the morning
  and dwell in the uttermost parts of
    the sea,
even there thy hand shall lead me,
  and thy right hand shall hold me.
If I say, "Let only darkness cover me,
  and the light about me be night,"
even the darkness is not dark to thee,
  the night is bright as the day,
  for darkness is as light with thee.

For thou didst form my inward parts,
  thou didst knit me together in my
    mother's womb.
I praise thee, for thou art fearful and
    wonderful.
  Wonderful are thy works!
Thou knowest me right well.

my frame was not hidden from thee,
when I was being made in secret,
    intricately wrought in the depths of the
      earth.
(Psalm 139:4-15)

The impersonal absolute of Plotinus and of so many modern Christians cannot be fitted unto the Holy Spirit of prophet or priest.

EIGHT
The Spirit in the Gospels

Christ and John the Baptist

The first gift the Holy Spirit gives for the new order established by Christ is Christ himself. To Mary of Nazareth, the angel announced, "The Holy Spirit will come upon you, and the power of the Most High will overshadow you; therefore the child to be born will be called holy, the Son of God" (Luke 1:35).

To Joseph, her husband, the angel said, "Do not fear to take Mary your wife, for that which is conceived in her is of the Holy Spirit" (Matthew 1:20).

Mary visited her kinswoman Elizabeth, pregnant with the child who was to be John the Baptist. When Elizabeth heard the greeting of Mary, the babe leaped in her womb, and Elizabeth was filled with the Holy Spirit. It is an interesting fact that the same Greek verb is used for the baby's leaping in the womb as for David's dancing before the ark (2 Samuel 6:16). David leaped before God's written word; John leaped before the Word himself.

PART II | THE SPIRIT IN ACTION

This was the first meeting, so to speak, of the cousins John and Jesus. The second was a real confrontation, vital for both, vital for us in our need to see Jesus closer and clearer. For this is the first time we meet him as a grown man. Of how he had spent the nearly twenty years after his parents found him in the temple—of what his development was, his hopes and fears, we know nothing. We know more about John. He had been in the region around the Jordan "preaching a baptism of repentance for the forgiveness of sins" (Luke 3:3). People wondered if he might be the Christ. He answered, "I baptize you with water for repentance, but he who is coming after me is mightier than I. . . . He will baptize you with the Holy Spirit and with fire" (Matthew 3:11).

And Jesus presented himself at the River Jordan for baptism by John.

This is one of the rare happenings to be found in all four gospels. It would be folly to write it off as incomprehensible. Certainly the coming of Jesus for baptism startled, almost shocked, the Baptist: "I need to be baptized by you, and do you come to me?" Jesus answered, "Let it be so now; for thus it is fitting for us to fulfil all righteousness" (Matthew 3:14-15). We can theorize, but with little confidence. With the term "righteousness," Jesus seems to be saying that if John did not baptize him, there would be some requirement of justice that had not been met, either in himself or in the work he had come into the world to do.

John's baptism was not the sacrament of water and the Holy Spirit of which Jesus had spoken to Nicodemus; it was a token of repentance, cleansing therefore to the soul, but not a rebirth. But when Jesus came up from the water he saw the Spirit. God descended on him in the form of a dove, a light shone on him, and he heard a voice from heaven saying, "This is my beloved Son, with whom I am well pleased" (Matthew 3:17). So water and the Holy Spirit were present.

Twice the Baptist bore witness that something of vast importance had happened. The first time, John said, "I saw the Spirit descend as a dove from heaven, and it remained on him. I myself did not know him; but he who sent me to baptize with water said to me, 'He on whom you see the Spirit descend and remain, this is he who baptizes with the Holy Spirit.' And I have seen and have borne witness that this is the Son of God" (John 1:32-34).

The next day the Baptist was standing with two of his own disciples, Andrew and John. He looked at Jesus walking nearby and said, "Behold, the Lamb of God." The two disciples, hearing this, followed Jesus (John 1:35-37). It was the first movement away from John to

Jesus, which causes John to say not so long after, "I am not the Christ, but I have been sent before him. . . . He must increase, but I must decrease" (3:28-30). Given the relationship of the two mothers, we might have expected more to be said by both the sons!

Jesus, Full of the Spirit

What indeed did it all mean to Jesus himself? Again we must walk warily. We must not think that we can read the mind of a God-man, real as his manhood is, as we know the mind of men conceived as we were ourselves. Yet it must have been bliss for him to hear of the Father's joy in him. What servant of God is ever satisfied with his own obedience; what lover of God with his own love? And what he had received was a combination of water and the Holy Spirit, which was to be his own description of baptism. We cannot know what that might mean in one whose conception was by the Holy Spirit. But we do know, because he said so, that it fulfilled all righteousness.

His human soul and his human body were created; so are ours. They needed sanctifying grace, as ours do, if they were to have the life-above-nature in union with God here and hereafter. The grace was there from his conception. It may have come, as ours comes, from the

Holy Spirit. It may, for all we know, have come from the union of his humanity with the Second Person of the Trinity—the union theologians call "hypostatic." But in mankind, the flow of grace is the other way—from nature to person. And Jesus does not use his person to bypass his nature.

At any rate, after the descent of the dove, Jesus, "full of the Holy Spirit, returned from the Jordan, and was led by the Spirit for forty days in the wilderness, tempted by the devil" (Luke 4:1-2). Matthew sees the temptation by the devil as the purpose of the Spirit's leading him there. Mark puts the "leading" more strongly: "The Spirit immediately drove him out [*ekballei*] into the wilderness" (Mark 1:12).

For those who dismiss the devil as no more than an odd fossil remain of Judaism, which even Jews have long outgrown, Christ's concern with Satan is a continuing irritant. His references to Satan cannot simply be penciled out. Too much in the gospels grows out of them and would be pointless without them.

The most spectacular instance, perhaps, is Jesus' reaction to the accusation that he casts out demons by the power of Satan. He retorts vehemently and in two ways. First he says that he casts them out "by the finger of God," which means that "the kingdom of God has come upon you" (Luke 11:20). Then he adds that the denial of the Holy Spirit is the worst of sins: "Truly, I say to you, all sins will be forgiven the sons of men, and whatever blasphemies they utter; but whoever blasphemes against the Holy Spirit never has forgiveness, but is guilty of an eternal sin" (Mark 3:28). Matthew phrases it, "will not be forgiven, either in this age or in the age to come" (Matthew 12:32). Learned men have pondered what the unforgivable sin is. John Bunyan's fear that he himself had committed it brought him to the point of madness. The ordinary theological teaching is that the sin against the Holy Spirit is to die in one's sins without repentance. Final refusal of God's love eliminates the work of the Spirit, because it is by the way of love that the Holy Spirit subsists and functions in us.

It is this "Jesus, full of the Spirit," that we are to meet in the rest of the gospel. Thus we find him after the temptations returning "in the power of the Spirit into Galilee" (Luke 4:14). Standing up to read in the synagogue at Nazareth, he was given Isaiah and found the place where it is written,

> "The Spirit of the Lord is upon me,
> because he has anointed me to preach
> good news to the poor.
> He has sent me to proclaim release to

> the captives
> and recovering of sight to the blind,
> to set at liberty those who are oppressed,
> to proclaim the acceptable year of the
> Lord."
> (Luke 4:18-19)

At that, Jesus closed the book, sat down, and said, "Today this scripture has been fulfilled in your hearing" (Luke 4:21).

So far, the congregation was pleased with him, though wondering where he got his learning (hardly at the village school, one imagines). But then he went on to talk of Elijah's feeding of one gentile and healing of another. The spell was broken. They led him to the brow of a hill over which Nazareth was built, so that they might hurl him to his death. But, "passing through the midst of them, he went away" (Luke 4:30).

An Indwelling

John's sixth chapter, on the feeding of the five thousand and Christ's teaching on himself as the bread of life, everyone knows. Not so well known is the seventh. On the relationship of Jesus, and so of us, to the Holy Spirit, it is beyond price.

It begins with the cousins of Jesus, who with the other Mary, their mother (Matthew 27:55-56), seem to have formed one household with Jesus and his mother. They were urging him to go to Jerusalem with them for the feast of the Tabernacles. In the great city, they argued, thousands would see his miracles. "Even his brethren did not believe in him," John remarks (John 7:5), but they knew he could work miracles, and that power could be exploited: they would be his public relations men.

Jesus answered, "I am not going up to this feast, for my time has not yet fully come" (John 7:8). So his brethren went to the feast without him. "Then, he also went up, not publicly, but in private" (7:10). We are reminded of the wedding feast in Cana. There also he said that his time had not yet come, but he changed the water into wine all the same. In our present instance the careless reader might see a contradiction, but going up for the feast is not the same thing as going to Jerusalem during the feast, and we are not told of his taking any part in the celebration.

May there not have been a special reason for his going? The Spirit, who had brought the prophet Ezekiel to Chaldea (Ezekiel 11:24) and Jesus to the desert, might have sent him to Jerusalem at that moment. It is natural for us to speculate as to why Jesus does the unexpected; but it is unsafe to omit the possibility that the Spirit may have guided him for reasons we cannot know. If we do omit it, we are in danger of merely deciding what we would have done, which casts light upon us, but not necessarily upon him.

What we do know is that Jesus was filled with the Spirit, and that what he did in Jerusalem was what the Spirit might have rather especially wanted done. The feast had begun centuries earlier to celebrate the harvest but had come more and more to be concerned with water, the water the farmers needed. In both Testaments water is a symbol of the Holy Spirit. We have already heard Jesus say to the woman at the well in Samaria, "Whoever drinks of the water that I shall give him will never thirst; the water that I shall give him will become in him a spring of water welling up to eternal life" (John 4:14).

On the last day of the feast, there was a spectacular ritual. On that day, "the great day," says John, Jesus cried out, "If any one thirst, let him come to me and drink. He who believes in me, as the scripture has said, 'Out of his heart shall flow rivers of living water'" (John 7:37-38).

What had Scripture said? The references are plentiful to water as a symbol of the Holy Spirit. Perhaps the clearest is Isaiah 44:3, where God says, "I will pour water on the thirsty land, and streams on the dry ground; I will pour my Spirit upon your descendants, and my blessing on your offspring."

John comments (John 7:39), "Now this he said about the Spirit, which those who believed in him were to receive; for as yet the Spirit had not been given, because Jesus was not yet glorified." There are two problems here: first, the Spirit had not yet been given, and second, Jesus had not yet been glorified.

We consider the second problem first. It is part of the mystery of the incarnation and does not directly concern the Holy Spirit, who is our topic. For a brief answer we go to the letter to the Hebrews. Verse 10 of the second chapter says, "It was fitting that he [God], for whom and by whom all things exist, in bringing many sons to glory, should make the pioneer of their salvation perfect through suffering." And in verse 18 we read, "For because he himself has suffered and been tempted, he is able to help those who are tempted." This statement that Christ himself must be made perfect through suffering is told us again, even more clearly, at Hebrews 5:8-9: "Although he was a Son, he learned obedience through what he suffered; and being made perfect he became the source of eternal salvation to all who obey him." To be told that Christ "learned obedience" does not mean that he, who loved to do the will of his Father, had been disobedient. But there is what we may call "a fourth dimension of obedience" for those who have suffered agony and death for it. In that lay the "perfection" in which Christ could take his place at the Father's right hand as head of a new humanity.

But what of John's comment that "the Spirit had not yet been given" (John 7:39)? There were the comings of the Spirit in the Old Testament; and we remember that the Baptist's parents had been filled with the Holy Spirit, as was Simeon who took the child Jesus in his arms in the temple, to say nothing of Mary upon whom the Holy Spirit came when she conceived Jesus. Then, of course, there was Jesus himself.

What the Spirit may have done in the souls of Jesus and Mary passes anything on which our experience can cast light. But for the rest, it seems clear that Christ's work of renewal does not exclude the presence of the Holy Spirit in mankind. That presence had been there always. Jesus would make it new. Through him it would be an indwelling.

In the past, the Spirit had given all sorts of aid, but he had not given himself. He had given men and women light and strength. But indwelling, abiding in them—this is something new. The Holy Spirit, as he dwelled in the soul of Christ made perfect by suffering, would henceforth make his home in us. It may be an oversimplification to say that the Holy Spirit had been giving (as he still gives) what the theologians call actual graces—impulses that, if we respond to them, give sanctifying grace. But, as we have seen, indwelling has a new depth and permanence.

Permanence? Salvation is involved in this indwelling of the Spirit. The Spirit will not withdraw, but we may refuse to keep our hold on him. Our Lord gives solemn warnings to those who lead others astray, and to those who go their own way against his.

For the first sort, those who cause others to sin, his condemnation is somber: "It would be better for him to have a great millstone fastened round his neck and to be drowned in the depth of the sea" (Matthew 18:6).

For the others who fell away, Jesus has a plea rather than condemnation. He speaks of a beginning of sorrows. "They will deliver you up to tribulation, and put you to death; and you will be hated by all nations for my name's sake. And then many will fall away, and betray one another, and hate one another. . . . And most men's love will grow cold. But he who endures to the end will be saved" (Matthew 24:9-10, 12-13).

Happy are we if none of this happens to us. But, like God, we must hate the sin but love the sinner. It was near the end of his own life that the French novelist

François Mauriac strained words to their limit in uttering what this meant to him: God wants us to be good,
will help us to be good, but he does not withhold his
love until we become good. "God loves me as I have
been, as I am, as I detest myself for being."

It would be hard to put more of the gospel into one
sentence.

NINE

The Spirit in the Church's Beginning

Jesus, we remember, handed over his church on earth to the keeping of the Holy Spirit, who had guided him in his founding of it. Not that by this we have lost anything of Jesus, except only his bodily presence as the apostles had had it for the two years before his death and the forty days after his resurrection. Indeed, as members of Jesus' mystical body, the church, we are closer to him, "indwelled" by him as they had never been.

All that comes to us flows from this membership in his body. The most priceless gift that flows from it is the Holy Spirit's dwelling in us as he dwells in Christ, acting on us as on Christ. This is not a matter of a choice or chance, you understand—as if we might have been given Jesus but were given the Spirit instead. We have Jesus by having the Spirit dwelling in us as in him. That is why the Holy Spirit is sometimes called "the Spirit of Jesus" or "the Spirit of the Lord." Jesus had told the apostles that if he did not go, the Holy Spirit would not come. In his first Pentecost sermon, Peter told the crowd what had happened. Jesus, having been raised by God, "being therefore exalted at the right hand of God, and having received from the Father the promise of the Holy Spirit, . . . has poured out this which you see and hear" (Acts 2:33).

The great pouring came at Pentecost with "tongues as of fire, distributed and resting on each one of them. And they were all filled with the Holy Spirit" (Acts 2:3-4).

Examples from the Early Church

At the beginning of this book we saw something of the handover of the church by Jesus and the take-over by the Holy Spirit. It is worth noting a few more instances of the action of the Spirit in the early church, remembering that the intervention of the Holy Spirit is practically continuous.

Antioch soon emerged as another center of activity. There Christ's followers were first called Christians. From Antioch, Barnabas and Paul, sent by the Holy Spirit, went to Seleucia and on to Cyprus, where they were joined by John (Acts 13:4-5). On a second journey, Paul and Timothy "went through the region of Phrygia and Galatia, having been forbidden by the Holy Spirit to speak the word in Asia. . . . They attempted to go into Bithynia, but the Spirit of Jesus did not allow them" (16:6-7).

Explaining to the elders of the church in Ephesus why he had sailed past their city, Paul said, "I am going to Jerusalem, bound in the Spirit, not knowing what shall befall me there; except that the Holy Spirit testifies to me in every city that imprisonment and afflictions await me" (Acts 20:22-23).

Paul's words are a sober reminder that the activity of the Spirit in us is not just for one's personal enjoyment or enrichment. The world needs Christ's message, and our willingness to give it is a supreme test of the reality of the Spirit's presence in ourselves. It was "full of the Holy Spirit" that Stephen went to his martyrdom (Acts 7:55). It was because he chose to "lie to the Holy Spirit" on a matter of money that Ananias died ingloriously (5:3-5).

This may be a good moment to glance at a question that has arisen throughout this book: *how* does the Spirit communicate with us? How, for example, did the Spirit convey to Paul that he was not to go into Bithynia? We are not told. It was in a dream that the Spirit told Paul to go to Rome, but dreams figure rarely in the Spirit's communication. For the most part—with Paul, with Isaiah, with Ezekiel—it may have been verbal; it left them in no doubt. We shall come back later to the matter that concerns ourselves: how are *we* to recognize the messages of the Spirit for the conduct of our own lives?

A Personal God

What did it mean to the Spirit that he should find men and women and children in their millions and billions made in some sense his special province? There are moods in which we find speculating on the emotional life of God irresistible. And there can be value in it, provided we realize that the gap between ourselves and our creator cannot always be bridged by us with total certainty; his ways are unsearchable, but he wants us to search.

What did Father and Son mean to each other, for instance? Every instinct tells us that in God as in mankind, parenthood could not be simply a matter of begetting, of no further interest or consequence to either. With us it is a continuing relationship. The details of the relationship may change. Time changes both parent and child. But, unless it goes badly wrong, the bond is forever. In the matter of God the Father and the Son he generated, we are not left to our instincts. When we read of Jesus in Scripture, the Father is constantly present. Only once are we told of Jesus' actually saying, "I love the Father" (John 14:31), but it was as he was leaving the upper room for Gethsemane and Calvary. And in the very moment of death he prays, "Father, into your hands I commend my spirit."

Of the Father's love for the Son, we are told by John that God so loved the world that he gave his only begotten Son (John 3:16); by Paul that for our sakes he did not spare his own Son (Romans 8:32). Our love for one another is only a shadow of his, but the shadow is cast by his.

Our relationship with the Spirit too is personal, not just official, so to speak. Scripture gives us two extraordinary statements, one about what we mean to God, one about what we mean to the Spirit. About God, James tells us that he "yearns jealously over the spirit which he has made to dwell in us" (James 4:5). About the Holy Spirit, Paul tells us that he "helps us in our weakness; for we do not know how to pray as we ought, but the Spirit himself intercedes for us with sighs too deep for words" (Romans 8:26). The Douay-Rheims version translates this last phrase as "unspeakable groanings." Either way, the meaning is clear. Helping mankind is not just a flick of the wrist for the Spirit: he cares. Our own sighing and groaning do rouse an echo in him, as our helplessness rouses a yearning in the Father.

Reactions of this sort are meaningless for the supreme being of Plotinus, a being utterly beyond any care for the all-but-nothings that we are in comparison with him. But Plotinus had not received God-made-man sacramentally; indeed, he would have rejected God-made-man with horror. He had arrived at his own God. We know that it could not mean to him what the God who has revealed himself means to us. Plotinus' impersonal god not only does not care about us; he does not even know about us. We are beneath his knowing. But we know better. We know that we are known and loved by God, because his Spirit dwells within us.

The Spirit of Truth

At the Last Supper, Christ told the apostles that when the Spirit of Truth came, he would lead them into all truth and bring to their memory all that he had taught them. The Acts of the Apostles and the New Testament letters and epistles are full of this progression deeper into truth. Paul writes:

> What God has prepared for those who love him, God has revealed to us through the Spirit. For the Spirit [for our sake!] searches everything, even the depths of God. . . . No one comprehends the thoughts of God except the Spirit of God. Now we

have received not the spirit of the world, but the Spirit which is from God, that we might understand the gifts bestowed on us by God. And we impart this in words not taught by human wisdom but taught by the Spirit. (1 Corinthians 2:9-13)

To have the words of God is wonderful, but "no prophecy of scripture is a matter of one's own interpretation, because no prophecy ever came by the impulse of man, but men moved by the Holy Spirit spoke from God" (2 Peter 1:20-21).

In Scripture, prophecy does not usually mean foretelling but "forth telling," telling the truth, especially God's truth. Here, as so often, it means teaching things vital to be known, too often forgotten. Prophecy is the work of the Spirit.

That we may know the truths God wants us to know is the special work of the Holy Spirit in the mystical body—truths about ourselves, for instance, some of which may make us rub our eyes. We may take calmly Paul's statement about the Christian community, "We are the temple of the living God; as God said, 'I will live in them and move among them'" (2 Corinthians 6:16). But if we are actually listening, we could be all but stunned by hearing Paul say the same thing about ourselves: "Do you not know that your body is a temple of the Holy Spirit within you?" (1 Corinthians 6:19). Just what have we been doing with our bodies? Paul goes on: "You are not your own, you were bought with a price" (6:19-20).

What the Holy Spirit Gives

At the baptism by John, the Holy Spirit descended on Jesus in the form of a dove. At Pentecost he descended on the disciples in the form of tongues as of fire resting upon each. The effect of both descents was the same. Christ was filled with the Holy Spirit at the Jordan, as were the disciples in the upper room—filled as a community and as individuals.

The Spirit's coming brought newness of life, gifts beyond measure, duties beyond bearing often enough— "those who belong to Christ have crucified the flesh" (but the flesh has its own power to crucify). Let us consider the gifts first—the greater gifts before the lesser, beginning with vision and its utterance. "No one can say 'Jesus is Lord' except by the Holy Spirit" (1 Corinthians 12:3).

Obviously anyone could utter those words. Paul is telling us that to say them and know what we are saying is a gift of the Holy Spirit. The God-man found guidance in the Spirit, and our need for guidance is not less than his.

We cannot get the whole picture of the Holy Spirit's gifts better than by reading the twelfth chapter of 1 Corinthians. Here is some of it:

> There are varieties of gifts, but the same Spirit; and there are varieties of service, but the same Lord; and there are varieties of working, but it is the same God who inspires them all in every one. To each is given the manifestation of the Spirit for the common good. To one is given through the Spirit the utterance of wisdom, and to another the utterance of knowledge according to the same Spirit, to another faith by the same Spirit, to another gifts of healing by the one Spirit, to another the working of miracles, to another prophecy, to another the ability to distinguish between spirits, to another various kinds of tongues, to another the interpretation of tongues. . . . By one Spirit we were all baptized into one body—Jews or Greeks, slaves or free— and all were made to drink of one Spirit. (1 Corinthians 12:4-10, 13)

Two things are to be noted about this list—one actually contained in it, the other implicit in it. Contained in it is the statement, "To each is given the manifestation of the Spirit for the common good." The gifts may enrich each recipient, yet that is not what they are primarily for. Their primary purpose is to enrich the whole church of Christ. Implicit in the list is the *warning* that we should not be greedy for the gifts: "Are all apostles? Are all prophets? Are all teachers? Do all work miracles?" (12:29). Instead, we are earnestly to desire the higher gifts. Paul goes on to explain this in chapter 13—the greatest panegyric of love ever written. It is a short chapter. It would be a pity not to know it by heart. It begins,

> If I speak in the tongues of men and of angels, but have not love, I am a noisy gong or a clanging cymbal. And if I have prophetic powers, and understand all mysteries and all knowledge, and if I have all faith, so as to remove mountains, but have not love, I am nothing. If I give away all I have, and if I deliver my body to be burned, but have not love, I gain nothing. (1 Corinthians 13:1-3)

Paul begins chapter 14: "Make love your aim, and earnestly desire the spiritual gifts, especially that you may prophesy." That is, teach the truths of God. Paul explains,

> He who speaks in a tongue edifies himself, but he who prophesies edifies the church. Now I want you all to speak in tongues, but even more to prophesy. . . . I thank God that I speak in tongues more than you all; nevertheless, . . . I would rather speak five words with my mind, in order to instruct others, than ten thousand words in a tongue. (1 Corinthians 14:4-5, 18-19)

Paul is not decrying tongues when he says, "Since you are eager for manifestations of the Spirit, strive to excel in building up the church" (1 Corinthians 14:12). He is reminding his listeners that the first words of Christ's final commission were "Go therefore and make disciples of all nations, . . . *teaching* them to observe all that I have commanded you" (Matthew 28:19-20).

"The fruit of the Spirit is love, joy, peace, patience, kindness, goodness, faithfulness, gentleness, self-control" (Galatians 5:22): The trouble is that all these virtues would be just about impossible without the aid of the Spirit, and we have countless ways of refusing his aid! Paul gives a warning of what may happen in fact—conceit, provoking one another, envy.

The Spirit knows us better than we know him, better than we know ourselves. We have been concentrating on his gifts. His demands tell us something of what he knows about *us*. Consider the duties he reminds us are ours.

"Guard the truth that has been entrusted to you by the Holy Spirit who dwells within us" (2 Timothy 1:14). This is another work of the Spirit that is not for ourselves only. "We are ambassadors for Christ, God making his appeal through us" (2 Corinthians 5:20). "You were called to freedom, brethren; only do not use your freedom as an opportunity for the flesh. . . . The whole law is fulfilled in one word, 'You shall love your neighbor as yourself'" (Galatians 5:13-14). Two verses later Paul writes, "Walk by the Spirit, and do not gratify the desires of the flesh. For the desires of the flesh are against the Spirit. . . . The works of the flesh are plain: immorality, impurity, licentiousness, idolatry, sorcery, enmity, strife, jealousy, anger, selfishness, dissension, party spirit, envy, drunkenness, carousing, *and the like*" (Galatians 5:16, 19).

"Do you not know that your bodies are members of Christ? Shall I therefore take the members of Christ and make them members of a prostitute?" (1 Corinthians

6:15). "Do not grieve the Holy Spirit of God, in whom you were sealed for the day of redemption" (Ephesians 4:30). The writer of that had surely read the verse of Isaiah (63:9-10) about the infidelities of the Jews: "In all their affliction he was afflicted . . . ; in his love and in his pity he redeemed them. . . . But they rebelled and grieved his holy Spirit."

I have not enough knowledge to say whether or not other Life–in-the-Spirit religions than Judeo-Christian have a God whose reaction to mankind's sinfulness is grief. The Holy Spirit is groaning, sorrowing. These are the reactions of love. Has any other religion said of its God as John said of our God—that "God is love" (1 John 4:8)?

As we have noted, God's love is not blind love. Knowing us for what we are, God loves us. It is out of love that he tells us of our "unloveliness," as it is not out of hatred that a doctor tells us of the evils that afflict our bodies. The apostle Jude repeats the warning (so does Matthew, among others): "'In the last time there will be scoffers, following their own ungodly passions.' It is these who set up divisions, worldly people, devoid of the Spirit" (Jude 18-19).

TEN
Life in the Spirit

The third chapter of John's gospel begins with Jesus telling Nicodemus that one cannot enter the kingdom of God unless he is born again. Nicodemus, learned Jew, Pharisee, member of the supreme Sanhedrin, could make no sense of this at all. Indeed it stirred him to mockery: was Jesus saying that a grown man must get back into his mother's womb and find his way out again? Wasting no time on the mockery, Jesus repeated, "Truly, truly, I say to you, unless one is born of water and the Spirit, he cannot enter the kingdom of God" (John 3:5).

Rebirth was not in the Old Testament. Now Nicodemus was being asked to believe, on the word of a carpenter from Nazareth, that without rebirth one *cannot* enter into the kingdom—in which, as a good Jew, he assumed he already was.

"Born again," said Jesus. The Greek term might also mean "born from on high." Either way, Jesus meant a second birth. Since birth is entry into life, a second birth is entry into a second life. "That which is born of the flesh," Jesus went on, "is flesh, and that which is born of the Spirit is spirit. Do not marvel that I said to you, 'You must be born anew'" (John 3:6-7).

Whenever Jesus tells us not to marvel, we must be ready for something at once very important and very surprising. "Born of the flesh" means born in the way of nature; by that birth we are all born into membership in the human race. By birth of the Spirit, we are reborn into membership in Christ. We live two lives. One is natural. The other is above nature—"from on high," "supernatural life" the church has come to call it.

We who have been baptizing and getting baptized for nineteen centuries take it for granted. The wonder has gone out of it. In many parts of the English-speaking Christian world, baptism is spoken of as "Christening." The pronunciation "chrissening" conceals the wonder of it (as "Crissmas" does of Christmas). If we would say it and think of it as *Christ*-ening, being Christed, made members of him, we should not take God-parenthood so casually. The same Spirit that "overshadowed" Christ's birth in Mary overshadows our birth in Christ and our god-child's.

Both lives—natural and supernatural—are real. The first empowers us to do things necessary if we are to exist and function as human beings at all. The second empowers us to live in a new relationship with God here on earth and to attain our maturity as men and women in union with God in heaven.

All One Body

"Membership in Christ" is not just a pious phrase. It has a definite meaning; salvation is in it. Jesus tells us that he is the life, so we beg him to live in us. But he also tells us that we must live *in him.* The Old Testament did little to prepare even learned Jews, which the apostles were not, for this two-way in-living—he in us, we in him. On his way to the garden of his agony, Jesus provided the key: "I am the vine, you are the branches. He who abides in me, and I in him, he it is that bears much fruit, for apart from me you can do nothing" (John 15:5). A vine does live—abide—*in,* pour its life into, its branches. But the branches live too—with the vine's life. Indeed the branches are necessary—no branches, no fruit. In the body that is Christ's church, the head cannot say to the feet, "I have no need of you" (1 Corinthians 12:21).

With Saul, on his way to Damascus to persecute Christians, our Lord has this dialogue:

"Saul, Saul, why do you persecute me?"
"Who are you, Lord?"

"I am Jesus of Nazareth whom you are persecuting."
(Acts 22:7-8)

By persecuting Christians, Paul was persecuting Christ himself. That identification of Christians with Christ himself never left Paul's mind. He generalized "vine and branches" into "body and members," or as we now say, "cells." The church is the body of Christ; Christ is the head, to whom, by the power of the Holy Spirit, we are joined. The essence of a body is that all the elements in it live by the one life—the life of the person whose body it is. Christ, risen from death, lives in us; we, reborn, live in him. He prayed for those who should come to believe in him, "that they may be one even as we are one, I in them and thou in me" (John 17:22-23).

The Two Lives

By nature we are a union of matter and spirit—body "ensouled," soul embodied. Those last four words are true of any living being with a material component, a body. We must not think that the words "soul" and "spirit" have the same meaning, are interchangeable. A soul is the life-principle in a body, human or animal or vegetable. A spirit is a being, not in space, that has abstract knowledge and love. Our bodies are "inlived" by a spiritual soul as no other body is; our spirit "inlives" a body as no other spirit does. If all this is not familiar to you, it will be profitable to let your mind dwell on it.

Having a spiritual soul, we know, love, decide. For knowing we have intellect, for loving and deciding we have will. We have memory, the power to recall things experienced. We have imagination, the power to relive things seen, heard, tasted, smelled, felt. We have emotions. (Imagination and emotion are priceless gifts, but loaded, as we all know, to our cost.)

The structure of natural life need not detain us. Our knowing power, our powers of love and decision, and the rest, are in constant use—the right use of any of them we call virtue. But the structure of life in the Holy Spirit—which is the permanently, everlastingly decisive life—does not lie so plainly under our gaze. Somehow we must harmonize the two lives; we must somehow get them to combine in one living reality.

It is not a matter of annihilating the life of nature and substituting life in the Spirit. The second life is built into the first: the same self functions in both, the same intellect studies mathematics and theology, the same "I" sins and repents, is tempted by the flesh, yet loves God.

This second life we call grace, *gratia* in Latin, *charis* in Greek. Both words mean "a free gift." Pause a moment on "free." Our natural life is given free of course. Before we came into existence we could do nothing to merit our bodies or our souls; indeed we were not there to receive a gift! But if God chose to make a human being, the elements simply belong. The life of grace is not demanded by our nature as human beings, except only in the negative sense that by our natural powers we could not in any event have reached the total union with God that in his love he wants us to reach. Given the damaged condition to which the human race reduced itself, God could have accepted mankind's choice of its own will against his and left us in our destitution. He chose freely to offer us a way up—a way that for his Son involved freely accepting death for us.

The first life has a structure; so has the second. Each life has powers and virtues proper to it; each has laws for the right use of its energies. In each, freedom consists in knowing the laws and living by them. Every element in our nature is called upon to function supernaturally too. Thus it is the function of the intellect to know and to grow in knowledge by applying judgment to all that comes pouring into it through the senses. By the virtue of *faith*, it is elevated to a new level of knowledge, accepting whatever God reveals because he reveals it.

By nature the will is attracted to whatever seems good to us, and we make our choices and decide our actions accordingly. By grace it is given the virtue St. Paul calls *charity*: our will is in a new contact with God's, we love what God loves, with love of God and neighbor as the prime principle of our decisions and actions.

To will and intellect, elevated by grace, comes the virtue of *hope*: believing that God—known by *faith* and loved by *charity*—is the goal of our life, realizing that the goal is difficult (we "work out our salvation with fear and trembling," Paul warns us), but confident that by God's grace we can reach it.

Faith, hope, and charity—these make up the essential structure of human life in the Spirit. The church calls them the theological virtues for the reason that God himself is their object. All virtues involve doing God's will, but these are directly *about* God: by faith we believe God, our hope is to come to union with God, by charity we love God (which involves loving our neighbor because God loves him).

You may find yourself wondering if God can be an "object." No word we use about God can be adequate. At least when we say we love God (the first of our

Lord's two commands), God is the grammatical object. Jesus freely uses the same word about God and us: "God is a spirit and we must worship him in spirit." As you plunge deeper, you may find yourself outgrowing "object." But you must start with it or some substitute word to have any fingerhold on the reality you are trying to comprehend.

Next come the virtues that concern our relations with and dealings with the created world, with people and things. They are prudence, justice, temperance, and fortitude. We call them the moral virtues.

In ordinary speech, *prudence* is the cautious virtue, linked closely with self-interest, which is not obviously virtuous! But in the life of the Spirit, the word means that by grace we see situations as they really are, serious situations especially. There are times when, to a faith-enlightened vision, the prudent thing would be to accept martyrdom. When we are on trial before the powers of this world, Christ tells us that the Holy Spirit will show us what to say, and give us the strength to say it.

The other three moral virtues are ways of acting with prudence, that is, in a clear vision of things as they are. By *justice* we want all men to have what is due to them. Above all, we will not take to ourselves what others are entitled to. By *temperance* we control our desire to do things and have things that promise pleasures we are not entitled to have. By *fortitude* we face our fears of the consequences of doing what it is our duty to do.

"The Gifts of the Spirit"

The gifts mankind has received from the Holy Spirit are beyond counting, Christ himself being one of them. But the phrase "gifts of the Spirit" has come to be used by Catholics for the spiritual qualities that Isaiah said would be in the Messiah because "the Spirit of the LORD shall rest upon him" (11:2). Isaiah names six of them. The Septuagint makes it seven; because one Hebrew word can stand for both piety and fear of the Lord, it listed them both. Jerome's Vulgate followed the Septuagint. The church applies all seven gifts to us who are Christ's brothers and sisters. Spiritual writers have gone with all seven. I keep with the mainstream.

Understanding gives new eyes to the gift of faith, by which we accept what God has taught because he has taught it. What do the actual words God uses mean? What other truths issue from them? By the gift of understanding, the Spirit gives us light.

Wisdom and *Knowledge* teach the soul to respond to spiritual values ("He shall not judge by what his eyes see, or decide by or what his ears hear," Isaiah

11:3). Wisdom concerns God; knowledge concerns all that God has created.

Counsel is close to conscience. It guides the decisions we are to make and the steps we are to take, here and now, as problems arise. As understanding gives eyes to faith, counsel gives eyes to prudence. Among other things, it makes us aware of problems that might not have occurred to us.

Fortitude has to do with the moral virtue of the same name; it helps us to do right at whatever cost to ourselves.

Fear of the Lord is not panic fear but awe—the awareness of his all-holiness. It is close to temperance, especially in relation to the cravings of the flesh. "Pierce my flesh with your spear, for I am afraid of your judgment." Fear of the Lord is fundamentally fear of our own weakness.

Piety is love between those who are already bound by reverence; it is the love of the instructed heart for God because of the reverence we owe him.

Given that we have the three theological virtues and the four moral virtues, what need is there of the seven gifts of the Spirit? To use a familiar illustration, they are like sails catching the winds of the Spirit. The spirit is like a wind blowing as it sees good (John 3:8). Even without sails, a boat will go where wind and sea take it. But who would not have sails?

What Cells Are For

So far we have been looking at the enrichment of our being as members of, cells in, Christ's body—indwelled by the Spirit as he is, responding to the life-stream that flows from the blessed Trinity to every element in the body.

But cells are *in* a body. They exist not for their own sake but to serve, to meet the needs of the one whose body it is. How do we serve the God-man? Why indeed should the God-man have a body composed of us? Enthroned in heaven, what can he want with it or us?

The immediate answer is that the work he did for men here on earth while he was with us will not cease while there are people on earth. What he did himself in his brief earthly life he does still through this body so mysteriously and marvelously his—that is, he still acts through us in whom he lives, through us who live in him. Grace is not a laborsaving device. God has no will to do for us what we could do for ourselves. He could have done his redeeming work without enlisting co-workers, just as he could have brought us into existence without parents (as he seems to have done with angels).

Christ's mystical body is not a service station to which we resort for comfort and nourishment. We are part of it, with work to be done in it that he expects us to do. I hope this thought does not make you as uncomfortable as it makes me. I do not remember who reminded us that "we must not be delicate members of a thorn-crowned head."

So we face the reason for the body's existence—that Jesus may continue to work among men through it as he once worked in the body born of Mary. He said, "My Father is working still, and I am working" (John 5:17). What work did he do on earth?

He *taught*, of course, and he told us to go on teaching everybody, everywhere, till the end of time.

He *prayed*, and gave us a first lesson in prayer (Matthew 6:9-13; Luke 11:2-4).

He *mediated* between God and man, which Paul gives as the reason why we should pray for all men, kings and such especially (1 Timothy 2:1-5).

He *suffered*, and Paul can say, "In my flesh I complete *what is lacking* in Christ's afflictions for the sake of his body, that is, the church" (Colossians 1:24). It is a stunning phrase—something lacking in Christ's sufferings! In what he himself did, nothing is lacking. But God does not choose to do for men what they can do for themselves. We do not simply sit on the sidelines and watch Christ redeeming us. In the divine plan there is a value in suffering undergone by Christ's members in union with his. It is not an injunction to go and look for suffering; Christ did not; Paul did not. It means not shirking what we can and should be doing for him because of the suffering it might bring us. At all times, we should want his work to be done in the way he sees best, not slowing it down by our own refusal to take any part in it.

Delicate members? That kind of shirking would indeed be delicate. So would idleness, lifting no finger. So would merely luxuriating in spirituality, refusing to study Christ's message in order that others besides ourselves should receive the gifts of truth and life in the Spirit, which Jesus taught and prayed and suffered and died that all might have.

Two Lives at a Time

What casts a shadow on the splendor of our life in the Spirit is that the giving of this second, supernatural life does not annihilate the first, which is ours by birth. Grace is implanted in the beings we are by nature. We possess two lives with their powers and needs and desires. Our problem is to live so that they harmonize, so that they bring forth action that rightly expresses both. What we make of this problem is the measure of our value as human beings.

An illustration may make this clearer. Consider a man just baptized. By nature, let us suppose, he is a man of strong appetites, and he has gained the supernatural virtues of temperance, justice, and love of neighbor. Yet within a very short time of the ceremony, he finds himself absolutely aching for a woman. He goes to his place of business, and copes with the instincts that have driven him to success—no pity for competitors, the rights of others not even considered.

In the first flush of conversion he may control his sexual appetite, and his new understanding of the rights of others and the love due to them may stop him from seizing financial opportunities that once he would have snatched at. But it is hard to keep up conduct so much against the natural grain for month after month. You may expel nature with a pitchfork, says the Roman poet Horace, but back it comes.

Yet the gifts of love of neighbor, charity, justice, and temperance are real gifts, carrying with them real powers of action. But they are not automatic. God has made them possible, but we must make our own fight against the temptations that make them seem impossible.

There is an illustration I have found useful. A great musician playing on a damaged piano finds that he cannot produce great music. It is not enough to work on his musical gifts; he must get the piano tuned. We ourselves are the pianos that need tuning if the powers given to us by the Holy Spirit are to produce their music from us. It is not enough to multiply prayer and sacrament, though these are essential. We must work on ourselves, fighting if necessary to agony, against cravings, failing often enough but dusting ourselves off and trying again. The Holy Spirit will help us to do the right actions, but he will not do them for us. We cannot be saved without him, but he cannot save us without us, so to speak. Our salvation requires our response, a response that need not mean that we have succeeded, but must mean that we have tried. The battle is not lost while we still want to win it.

This is where the virtue of hope has its utmost practicality. The two main sins against hope, the church tells us, are presumption (taking our salvation for granted) and despair (thinking it impossible). Against a particular temptation, or any number of them, we may sink to despair. I think that is the point where the Spirit reinforces the power of hope. Naturally, our situation may seem and in a sense be hopeless; but, to use our Lord's words about the salvation of the rich, "What is impossible with men is possible with God" (Luke 18:27). That sentence is hope's charter. And along with hope comes a helping hand from faith: we have cost Christ so much that he will not let us damn ourselves while there is a spark of love still unextinguished in us. There is no place in hell for even the smallest flickering of love. There is no refusal in God, only in us. We constantly say no to him, but he does not easily take no for an answer.

The Holy Spirit will not force our will. But he will give what the church has called actual graces—light to our minds, energy to our wills, to make the necessary efforts and resistances. If we accept them, we shall have his life once more in us. In the traditional phrase, we shall be in a state of grace—sanctifying grace.

The Spirit's Will for Us

We have already looked at the question of how the Holy Spirit spoke to prophets and apostles—how, for example, he ordered Paul not to go into Bithynia. As we say, the prophets hardly gave us a very clear idea of the process. One wonders what experience made Paul aware of the Spirit's "unspeakable groanings." Yet it is easy to believe that the Spirit has his own ways of convincing men and women who have a mission to the world that he has spoken to them.

My concern is how he communicates with you and me, who have been given no such world mission. How

does he give light to our darkness and strength to the
wills with which we make our individual decisions?
May we not be deceiving ourselves?

The Circumcellions, the extreme section of the Don-
atists in Augustine's Africa, who forced strangers to
kill them by threatening to kill the strangers if they did
not, were certain that they were doing the will of God;
rivers of blood have been shed throughout the centuries in the same conviction that God wants it that way.
But my concern is still with the unbloodstained majority—commonplace Christians who, if they murdered,
would know they had committed a great sin, but who
for the most part have to make decisions only about
their own daily lives.

We have so much to guide us aright. The Holy Spirit living in us sent Christ into the world and lived in
him. In the gospels and epistles that the Spirit inspired
men to write, in the teachings of the church that Christ
founded, most of our problems have been stated and
light given on them. It is surprising how much is cov-
ered by the command to love our neighbor as ourselves,
and it is surprising how much wisdom can come from
priests in the confessional.

Yet self-deception remains a possibility against
which it is never safe to lower our guard. Human
speech is of such a sort that it is scarcely possible to

write or utter a sentence in which a second meaning might not be found. When we are craving to do some particular action in which in one way or another the Spirit has shown us to be wrong, we have an incredible skill at unearthing second meanings that tell us what we want to hear.

Even when there is no craving involved, the self can fool us. Reading Scripture, we get sudden insights into the meaning of certain scriptural texts and scenes. No one else seems to have seen what we see! Our idea may be true, or partly true, or mainly false: but it is ours. There is a real danger that our insights may grow into idols, larger than life and twice as supernatural!

The only remedy for self-run-wild is prayer, the prayer that is speaking, the prayer that is listening, the prayer that is the directing of life to God. We must be aware of the danger and ask the Holy Spirit to help us know what his will is for us: we must ask it, and mean it. May the Holy Spirit somehow supply the sincerity we find so difficult.

ELEVEN
The Air We Breathe

In a notable poem, Gerard Manley Hopkins compared the Blessed Virgin to the air we breathe—"wild air, world-mothering air." But the Holy Spirit *is* the air we breathe: the Blessed Virgin breathed it too, as did her child.

Father and Son have constructed a universe with a life of wonderful possibilities for us here on earth, and a reality wonderful beyond dreams for our eternity. But we ourselves must make the efforts and resistances that health in it demands. The first law of health is that we must breathe.

To repeat: the Holy Spirit, the divine breath, is the air without which those efforts and resistances will be beyond our powers. Heaven knows, we can feel that life is too much for us, that we can't go on. "Half in love with easeful Death," wrote Keats, so soon to find death from tuberculosis. Half in love? Suicides increase in numbers. For infants in the womb, laws exist for death on demand (not the infants' demand). Laws are already written and sure to be enacted providing death on demand for everybody.

That convinced unbelievers should feel like this is not so surprising. Born into an unpurposed world for no special reason, living for the time above their native nothingness and certain to be reabsorbed in it—it is hard for them to feel themselves anything more than accidents that happened to happen.

The vast majority of people are not convinced unbelievers. There is something in them that says no to all this death-talk. They may go either way, not necessarily opting for nothingness.

Christians also may go either way. A dear friend of mine, a believing Catholic, has just chosen death, under what pressure of agony I do not fully know. Please pray that God may hold her in his love. In a world threatened by chaos, death can present itself as an inviting solution—easeful death. Life can seem so dubiously worth living.

That is why in a devitalized age, under the same pressure as everyone else, we should give more mind to the Spirit of Life, the Holy Spirit, with whose life-giving activities both Testaments positively sparkle.

The difficulty we have to overcome in ourselves is that the Trinity and all the truths that flow from it call on us to use mental muscles that for most of us are not often called upon. Spirit is, naturally enough, so very spiritual! It is not in space; it has no shape or color;

imagination (our daily substitute for thinking) cannot picture it. We are left only with Alexander Pope's "insupportable fatigue of thought." The pains of the world can be reacted to with no mental effort at all. A child dying in agony is so real; the joys of heaven (which the child may soon experience) seem so remote.

And even within the Trinity, the Holy Spirit is so much harder to picture than the Son. The Spirit was not born in a stable, had no father or mother to seek him sorrowing for three days, agonized in no garden, hung on no cross. Nor do we, at least in the New Testament, find the Spirit working physical miracles. I do not know whether Christians generally ask him for them; I do not remember that I ever have. What he has to give goes to the spiritual upbuilding of the church, and to the spiritual upbuilding of each one of us. That is a mightier thing than any miracle of healing the sick or raising the dead. (One wonders if, as the days went by, Lazarus was glad to be back.)

Maturity consists in having our priorities right, in seeing the spiritual as mightier than the physical or temporal. The paralyzed man, who was lowered through the roof by his friends to get him close to the healer from Nazareth, might have been sick with disappointment to hear Christ say that his sins were forgiven—

and enchanted to be told to take up his bed and walk. I think about that man a lot.

We can sympathize, empathize with Christ, and learn much of how to cope with our troubles from seeing how he coped with his. For the Holy Spirit we must trust our minds. For images, we have only a dove and some points of fire.

The evidence on which we trust him is to be found in small books like this, which will have failed if one does not move on to the Bible. There is no substitute for the whole Bible. But, even if one did no more than look into every reference given in this present book, one might find the Bible opening into richer treasures. One might find the mind producing delights with which imagination's technicolor cannot compare.

Epilogue

It is noticeable that in both Testaments the Spirit is constantly spoken of but is never spoken to. This is natural in the Old Testament, where he is not shown as a distinct person. But, by the time of Acts and the letters and epistles, Christ had not only shown the Spirit for who and what he is, but the Spirit had given us Christ and the Scriptures, and the apostles themselves had experienced his taking over the direction of the churches.

The deepest truths take longest to grow into. Not always, of course. Saints have their own pace. St. Paul, for instance, prepared by watching and listening to Stephen's martyrdom, and responded to the confrontation with Christ on the Damascus road at extraordinary speed; within twenty years he began the New Testament by writing 1 Thessalonians! But for communities the pace is always slower.

Seven hundred years after Moses, the Jews returned from Babylon, at last and incurably monotheists. Four hundred years after that, a sufficient number of them, and great numbers of gentiles, had reached the point at which the incarnation and the Trinity could be revealed. In the centuries before them, Jews had become accustomed to the Spirit as God in action, to the Word as God in utterance.

It may be that, in the fact that the first Christians did not address the Spirit directly, we are meeting another example of the necessity to grow gradually from acceptance to familiarity. At least now we have prayers to him, hymns to him—hymns especially.

We always opened our Catholic Evidence Guild meetings under the open sky with the prayer, "Come, Holy Spirit, and fill the hearts of thy faithful. Enkindle within them the fire of thy love. Send forth thy Spirit and our hearts shall be created. And thou shalt renew the face of the earth." And in that last sentence, from Psalm 104, we were reminded of the meaning of what we were doing on the platform. Only the Holy Spirit can renew the face of the earth, but he does it by renewing our hearts!

We have splendid hymns to him, too. But the trouble with hymns is that there can be so special a pleasure in hearing our voices raised in song that we cannot so easily concentrate on the meaning of the words we are singing.

So, forgetting the tune, let us concentrate on the words of the *Veni Sancte Spiritus*, "Come Holy Spirit":

it is remarkable how much is contained in its thirty lines. Here is a rough prose translation. You could make a more musical one? So could I. The object is more to show how much there is for each of us in its listing of the Spirit's gifts:

Come Holy Spirit;
Send us from heaven
A ray of your light.

Come Father of the poor,
Come giver of gifts,
Come, shine in our hearts.

Most consoling of consolers,
Soul's welcome guest,
Pleasant coolness.

Rest in toil,
Heat made bearable,
Solace in our tears.

O most blessed light,
Fill the depths of hearts
Confident in you.

Without your power
There is nothing in man,
Nothing unstained.

Clean what is filthy in us,
Freshen what has withered,
Mend what is broken.

Relax our rigidity,
Warm our coldness,
Straighten our crookedness.

Give to your faithful,
Confident in you,
Your sevenfold gifts.

Grant us the reward of virtue,
Grant us to die in your grace,
Grant us joy without end.

And every element in that long list is the simple truth, there for our having.

We began with eleven apostles around the supper table. Throughout this book they have been in my mind, the first of the millions of us to have the experience of hearing the impossible and finding it true. Let us conclude with them.

Five of them gave their names to books of the New Testament—Matthew and John to gospels; Peter, the other James, and Jude to letters and epistles. They all tell of the Holy Spirit. Jude, who, as you will remember, asked a loaded question at the table, mentions the Spirit twice in his hundred-line letter (Jude 19-20). The second time he writes, "Pray in the Holy Spirit; keep yourselves in the love of God; wait for the mercy of our Lord Jesus Christ unto eternal life" (20-21)—thus giving us the Trinity—and leading off with the third member.